NATURAL KNITS

NATURAL
KNITS

25 unique designs in sumptuous alpaca, llama, merino wool and silk

Jane Ellison

COLLINS & BROWN

First published in the United Kingdom in 2011 by
Collins & Brown
10 Southcombe Street
London W14 0RA

An imprint of Anova Books Company Ltd

Photographs of knitwear by Annie Bundfuss
Peruvian photographs by Glen Pearson and Peter Mulley

ISBN 978-1-84340-566-5

A CIP catalogue for this book is available from the British Library.

10 9 8 7 6 5 4 3 2 1

Reproduction by Rival Colour Ltd, UK
Printed and bound by 1010 Printing International Ltd, China

This book can be ordered direct from the publisher at www.anovabooks.com

contents

introduction

For all my knitting books, I design with the philosophy of creating simple, easy patterns with no complicated abbreviations or techniques – just straightforward patterns that let the beautiful yarns shine through. They are patterns for the beginner and the experienced knitter that result in a classic handknit that should last for years to come.

My design inspiration starts with the beauty of the yarn. The designs reflect what I feel is the best use of a particular yarn. Some of the designs use a technique that slips the stitches to create a finished effect that looks similar to Fair Isle or intarsia but actually does not involve any of the complicated techniques associated with colourwork. As always, I try to create simple, and easy-to-follow knitting patterns.

When working out the designs, my first and only thought when choosing a stitch technique is:
"What is easiest to knit so that the garment is a joy to knit as well as being lovely to wear?"

I love knitting and feel it is something anyone, and everyone, can do. It isn't difficult, or complicated. It is enjoyable, fun, and relaxing. Knitting is the ultimate in individuality. The beauty of the simple designs with the exciting yarns is that it results in classic garments that will last for years – as well as creating unique additions to suit any style. I hope my designs will bring joy and happiness to those who knit, or to those who receive a garment as an everlasting gift of friendship and love.

As a creative person I find it exciting that, even if several knitters use the same pattern, each knitter will create an individual and unique garment. It is interesting that even the smallest change (like a different colour) can create something new and bespoke for you.

Sharing knitting stories and techniques with other knitters is fun. There is something lovely about sitting down together with other knitters and just chatting about different knitting styles, ideas, and techniques. With this in mind, for this book, I have included my thoughts on the design at the start of each pattern.

I hope you enjoy making beautiful garments with the high-quality Mirasol yarns, and to do so knowing that the purchase of the yarn supports such a worthwhile cause (see pages 8–11), makes it extra special.

It feels good that we can make a difference.

the Mirasol project

The Mirasol Project, named after a girl called Mirasol and all that she represents, was set up in 2006 by Michell and Company, who run the Mallkini Ranch. The company has always had the interests of its employees at heart but felt it was time to go one step further in trying to change their lives for the better.

Imagine life in the shallow air of the high Peruvian Andes, above Lake Titicaca, where temperatures reach more than 30 degrees in summer, the mountains are permanently covered in snow in winter, and the sierras are lashed with hail and biting winds. In such an environment Mirasol and her little brother Alex, help tend a flock of 350 alpaca – part of a herd of 3,000 at the Mallkini Ranch. As one of the disadvantaged Quechua-speaking people she lives with her family in a one room stone hut, without windows, or a door, and sleeps fully clothed to keep warm. Few of the Quechua people can read or write, and their health is very poor. There has been no escape from such relentless poverty. What was needed was a school.

THE MIRASOL YARN COLLECTION

Peru and the Quechua-speaking people have an ancient and rich heritage of textile artistry. The Mirasol Yarn Collection was started with the aim of raising enough money from the the sale of alpaca, wool, silk and organic cotton yarns, from Quechua and around the world, to support the Mirasol Project. If it wasn't for the yarn made from the animals tended for generations in the Peruvian highlands, we would not have this beautiful yarn and the money to finance the building and day-to-day running of a boarding school for the children of the alpaca shepherds.

The Mirasol Yarn Collection is based on the principles of fair trade, where producers receive a price that covers sustainable production plus an extra premium that is invested in social, or economic development projects. In this way, fair trade guarantees that disadvantaged producers in the developing world get a better deal for their products. Every ball or hank bought from the Mirasol Yarn Collection contributes toward the Mirasol Project.

Although adding to the cost, the school has a boarding facility – this is vitally important because the children's families often live ten or more miles away from the ranch and attendance at the school would otherwise be impossible. The idea is for the children to stay at the school during the week and return home at weekends. So far everything has gone according to plan. Classrooms and dormitories, using local materials, have been built for the boys and girls as well as accommodation for the teaching staff and cook. There has been so much to think about: a clean water supply has been established; the kitchen equipped; linen for the beds purchased; exercise books and pencils chosen – even warm fleece school uniforms and pyjamas have been provided. The project is very important because currently Quechua-speaking children lag behind their contemporaries in school at all levels because the teaching is conducted in Spanish.

The aim of the Mirasol school is to make up for those differences and enable the children to reach a standard of educational excellence. One of the ways of achieving this is that here the children are being taught in both Quechua and Spanish. As well as an awareness of other cultures, there is an emphasis on the preservation of the language and customs of the children and their families. Realistic career opportunities are highlighted, and training is given in local skills such as trout farming, market gardening, the breeding and care of guinea pigs as a food source, traditional textile arts, and languages. Alongside these provisions, more lofty ideals are in place where the school fosters the principles of peace, tolerance, and equality with a respect for human rights and basic freedoms. The school is a place where children can develop personal, occupational and communication skills.

MAKING A DIFFERENCE
The school was officially opened on 11 March 2008 to much rejoicing. The whole building was decorated with coloured balloons and the classrooms were festooned with banners and drawings made by the children.

Raul Rivera for Michell and Company comments:
> *"It has taken us just three years to fulfil a dream that we hardly dared believe in, but time and time again we are shown that dreams can be fulfilled. If you really want something you can move a mountain."*

The school, and its ideals, has captured the imagination of many. The children are happy to entertain guests at the school, many from overseas, and are eager to learn something of their cultures. The guests bring gifts ranging from educational materials, to bicycles, and a gas

refrigerator. Stella Maris, an association of wives of the Peruvian Marine Force based at Lake Titicaca, gave each child a kit of personal items: a towel; soap; toothbrush and paste. The children were very excited by such a gift as personal hygiene items are a novelty. It seems everyone wants to help.

Jeffrey J. Denecke Jr., of Knitting Fever, the US Distributor of Mirasol Yarns, explains what involvement in the project has meant to him:

> "Becoming a part of the Mirasol Project brought home the harsh reality of faraway places where there is a lack of even the most basic necessities such as food, shelter, drinking water, education and health care. It has also made me more conscious of how powerful a tool money can be. How even a little bit can go such a long way in helping others less fortunate, knowing the tremendous impact our efforts have had on these children."

Alex, Mirasol's young brother, wrote a poem to celebrate the opening of the school. Here are a few lines:

Today I have new pencils,
And little pencils of colour,
What shall I draw with them?
A butterfly and a flower,
Long live the friends who help us,
Long live the Mirasol School at
 Mallkini!

We will leave what the children feel about their new life to 14 year-old Wilian Chunga:

> "I come from my house to the Mirasol Boarding House. I feel good here. I learn many things and study and do my homework. The teachers are very nice. I eat food with vitamins and proteins in order to grow strong and healthy and be able to be the first. This is why I love the Mirasol Boarding House. I never dreamed of living in a house that seemed God's house because I learn many things I didn't know before. This encourages me to go on with my studies. I appreciate this with all my heart. I also thank the persons who made this possible. I send them a big hug and wish them all happiness.
> Thank you!"

the Mirasol project

11

the Mirasol yarns used in this book

A couple of years ago, I was lucky to be able to visit the remote area that inspired the Mirasol Project. This journey made me really appreciate how much we take for granted and allowed me to experience the stunning scenery and ever changing climate of the region first hand. The light changed constantly from early morning sunrises to brilliant sunshine often mixed with rain or even hail. The distinct nature of the light and the changing weather, combine to create this climate and are mirrored in the Mirasol yarns. Each one produces a completely different look and feel – yet they all work well as a collection together.

For results that look like the projects featured in the photographs, always use the Mirasol yarn or yarns specified in the knitting pattern. The Mirasol Yarn Collection is constantly seeking new and exciting yarns to tempt us with, but sadly, they can only invest in a limited number of products and shades each year. This means that yarns and shades may not be available when you come to knit a project from this book. The following yarn descriptions have been compiled to help you find a substitute yarn, if necessary. Match the tension (gauge) as closely as possible and check the meterage. This will allow you to work out the quantity required of any potential substitute yarn. And, it is not unknown for yarn or shades to be reintroduced at a later date.

MISKI

Quechua meaning: fertile valley of Qhochapampa, conquered by Inka Ruka.
There aren't any words to describe Miski – and do it justice. It is the finest baby llama yarn that there ever has been (I might be very biased!). At first glance, the colours

seem straightforward: navy, orange or lilac. However, a closer inspection reveals that the shades are made up of three or four different colours creating a bejewelled appearance.
Length: 91yds (75m). **Fibre content:** 100% baby llama. **Stitches:** 18. **Needle size:** 5mm (US8). **Weight:** 50g (1¾oz).

AKAPANA

Quechua meaning: clouds, colouring of the sky at dawn or dusk.
Akapana is a deliciously, soft yarn inspired by tweeds – yet softened with baby llama. It is made up of two strands of varying thickness, plied together. It is composed of baby llama, merino wool and Donegal – in natural or multicoloured kneps.
Length: 87m (95yds). **Fibre content:** 65% baby llama, 25% merino wool, 10% Donegal. **Stitches:** 20. **Needle size:** 4.5mm (US7). **Weight:** 50g (1¾oz).

K'ACHA

Quechua meaning: messenger.
The beautiful combination of fibres create a luxiurious yarn that knits smoothly onto the

needles. The K'achais a roving yarn, hand painted in tone-to-tone colours composed of fine merino wool, suri alpaca and silk.

Length: 90m (98yds). **Fibre content:** 60% fine merino wool, 25% suri alpaca, 15% silk. **Stitches:** 20. **Needle size:** 4mm (US6). **Weight:** 50g (1¾oz).

QINA

Quechua meaning: reed pipe, flute, bamboo flute.

This is a simple combination of fibres that creates a classic favourite and is a joy to knit. The Bamboo comes from China and it is organic.

Length: 83m (91yds). **Fibre content:** 80% baby alpaca, 20% bamboo. **Stitches:** 20. **Needle size:** 4mm (US6). **Weight:** 50g (1¾oz).

SULKA

The silk gives the yarn a gorgeous sheen, which combined with the exquisite colours make this an enchanting yarn that a knitter may get addicted to. Like Miski, Sulka is a melange and each time I knit with it I see flecks or jewels of new colour.

Length: 50m (55yds). **Fibre content:** 60% merino wool, 20% alpaca, 20% silk. **Stitches:** 16. **Needle size:** 6mm (US10). **Weight:** 50g (1¾oz).

TUPA

Quechua meaning: something noble, something worthy, something of exceptional quality.

Tupa has a twist that allows the silk to shine through.

Length: 125m (137yds). **Fibre content:** 50% merino wool, 50% silk. **Stitches:** 22. **Needle size:** 4mm (US6). **Weight:** 50g (1¾oz).

HACHO

The yarn is unique in that it provides the warmth of merino wool but has a crispness that reminds me of soft cotton. It is hand dyed to create the painted look that makes this yarn unique. Tupa is a single shade alternative for all the Hacho patterns.

Length: 125m (137yds). **Fibre content:** 60% wool, 30% cashmere, 10% nylon. **Stitches:** 22. **Needle size:** 4mm (US6) **Weight:** 50g (1¾oz).

NUNA

Quechua meaning: soul, spirit, conscience.

Nuna is so luxuriously soft to knit with, almost delicate – but it has a strength. The merino wool gives the yarn elasticity, which makes it a very forgiving yarn to knit with if your stitches are a little uneven – wool eases them into uniformity! The silk accepts the dye beautifully and gives the yarn that lovely deep shade, as well as a deep shine. The bamboo in Nuna isn't dyed and gives the yarn its individuality.

Length: 175m (191yds). **Fibre content:** 40% merino wool, 40% silk, 20% bamboo. **Stitches:** 24. **Needle size:** 3.25mm (US5) **Weight:** 50g (1¾oz).

SAMP'A

Quechua meaning: light, soft, delicate, humble.

The Quechua meaning describes the yarn perfectly. Even though as a cotton it has strength, the way it is grown and dyed makes it a very delicate yarn.

Samp'a is a 100% organic cotton that is spun in Holland. All the shades are naturally dyed.

Length: 110m 120yds **Fibre content:** 100% naturally dyed organic cotton. **Stitches:** 22. **Needle size:** 4mm (US6). **Weight:** 50g (1¾oz).

All the dyestuffs used in production of the yarns are AZO-Free (except Samp'a which is made in Holland but is naturally dyed). All the yarns in the Mirasol Collection have Quechua names – the local dialect of the Quechua people.

reading patterns

SKILL LEVEL

I love knitting and I am always excited by the technique and actual knitting, just as much as the satisfaction of creating a bespoke garment. With this in mind I want other people to share my joy of knitting. My patterns are simple, straightforward and easy to follow and result in beautiful, classic garments.

MATERIALS AND NEEDLES

These indicate what you will need to complete the garment. However, the quantities of yarn are based on average requirements and therefore are approximate. The needle size is only a recommendation, you may have to change the needle size to get the correct tension (gauge).

MEASUREMENT AND SIZING INFORMATION

Everyone has a unique body shape. Before starting your garment, please check the "actual measurement" to make sure you are making the perfect size.

Each pattern includes a size guide, "to fit bust", and actual measurements which indicate the garment's length and width. Compare the measurements of a similar, well fitting garment in your closet, with the actual measurements stated in the pattern – choose the nearest pattern size.

ADJUSTING THE LENGTH

Ask a friend to measure your back from the top of your shoulder to your desired length or measure a favorite garment. Compare this length with the one in the pattern. Then,

work more or less rows before the Shape Armhole instruction on all the body pieces

The same principle applies to the sleeves. Once you have knitted the back and front, pin the shoulders and side seams together and put the garment shell on. Ask a friend to measure the distance from the top of the side seam to your desired sleeve length. To lengthen or shorten the sleeve, find he instruction in the pattern that states "Continue in pattern without shaping until sleeve measures [given length] from cast on edge", and use your preferred measurement. Remember when making your bespoke garment that you may require more or less yarn than stated.

TENSION (GAUGE)

Every pattern has it's own unique tension (gauge), represented as a number of stitches and rows counted over a 10cm (4ins.) square of knitted fabric in a stated stitch pattern. To make a tension (gauge) square, first cast on the number of stitches stated, then cast on an extra four stitches. Work in the stitch pattern stated, until the square measures 12cm (4¾ins.). Do not cast (bind) off but cut the yarn and thread the tail through the stitches, taking the stitches off the needle as you do so.

To calculate the tension (gauge), lay the square down flat, place pins to the side of a stitch near one side edge, and a second pin above a stitch near either the top or bottom edge. Using a tape measure or metal ruler, measure 10cm (4ins.) across the square from each pin and mark with two more pins. Count the number of stitches and rows between the pins. If you have the stated number of stitches and rows between the pins you have the correct tension (gauge) and can commence your chosen pattern. If you have too many stitches, your tension (gauge) is tight. Change to a larger needle. If there are too few stitches, your tension (gauge) is loose. Change to a smaller needle. Repeat and work another square until you achieve the correct tension (gauge).

STARTING TO KNIT

If you are comfortable with the techniques you use in knitting then please continue to use them. Knitting is about finding your own enjoyment and comfort with the needles, but below are my suggestions:

Casting on

I use the thumb method – this gives a good, elastic edge.

Decreasing

I use the following to create the necklines and armholes.

K2tog or p2togtbl: generally, I use these decreases at the end of a row.

K2togtbl or sl1, k1, psso or p2tog: generally, I use these decreases at the beginning of a row.

I work decreases one stitch in from the edge.

Joining in a new ball

It is better to join in a new ball at the beginning of a row. Gently twist the new ball with the old ball at the start of the row. If you are at the end of the row, tie the two ends in a knot. The ends can be sewn into the seams at the finishing stage.

Stripes

All my stripes are worked so that the yarn not being used can be carried up the side. Remember not to pull the yarn too tightly up the side – this can distort the knitting.

Casting (binding) off

Cast (bind) off loosely and always in pattern.

abbreviations

Knitting has a language of its own. Instructions for making a knitted item are written with abbreviated terms, here are the ones I use in my book:

cm	centimetres
ins.	inch(es)
k	knit
m1	increase one stitch by knitting into the front and back of the next stitch
patt	pattern
p	purl
psso	pass slipped stitch over
rem	remaining
rep	repeat
rev	reverse
sl1	slip one stitch
sl2	slip two stitches
st(s)	stitch(es)
st st	stocking (stockinette) stitch, knit 1 row, purl 1 row
tbl	through back of loop
tog	together
yrn	yarn round needle or yarn over needle

In the patterns, the instructions are given for the smallest size, with larger sizes in round brackets. Where only one figure or instruction is given this applies to all sizes. Work all directions inside square brackets the number of times stated.

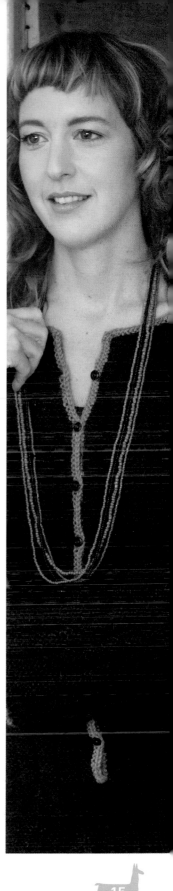

1

Cardigans and Jackets

short-sleeved, cropped cardigan
page 18

three-quarter sleeve, wrap cardigan
page 24

high collar, short-sleeved cardigan
page 29

long, ribbed, v-neck cardigan
page 34

cropped, v-neck cardigan
page 39

edge-to-edge lace and cable, chunky jacket
page 44

lace-ribbed, hooded jacket
page 49

three-quarter length, cable coat
page 55

HACHO
short-sleeved, cropped cardigan

The length of this round-neck cardigan with lace panels creates a fitted shape to complement any size.

MEASUREMENTS

To fit bust	81.5–86.5	86.5–91.5	96.5–101.5	106.5–112	117–122	cm
(suggested)	32–34	34–36	38–40	42–44	46–48	ins.
Actual	92	100	108	116	124.5	cm
measurement	36¼	39¼	42½	45½	49	ins.
Length	40	40	44	44	46	cm
	15¾	15¾	17¼	17¼	18	ins.
Sleeve length	7	7	8	8	9	cm
	2¾	2¾	3	3	3½	ins.

MATERIALS

5 (6, 6, 7, 7) 50g (1¾oz) hanks of Hacho
    or Tupa for a single shade alternative
(photographed in Hacho, Deep Blue Ocean,
shade 306)

8 (8, 8, 8, 9) small buttons

NEEDLES

One pair of 4mm (US6) knitting needles
One pair of 3.75mm (US5) knitting needles
Three stitch holders
Knitter's sewing needle or tapestry needle

TENSION (GAUGE)

22 stitches and 30 rows to 10cm (4ins.)
square over stocking (stockinette) stitch
using 4mm (US6) needles.

Back

With 3.75mm (US5) needles, cast on
101 (110, 119, 128, 137) stitches.

RIB PATTERN

Row 1 (right side): K2, [p2, k3, p2, k2]
to end.
Row 2: P2, [k2, p3, k2, p2] to end.
These 2 rows form the rib pattern.
Repeat the last 2 rows until back measures
5 (5, 6, 6, 7)cm (2 (2, 2¼, 2¼, 2¾)ins.)
ending with a wrong-side row.
Change to 4mm (US6) needles.
Starting with a purl row, work in reverse
stocking (stockinette) stitch until the back
measures 18 (18, 20, 20, 22)cm
(7 (7, 7¾, 7¾, 8¾)ins.) from cast-on
edge, ending with a wrong-side row.

SHAPE ARMHOLES

Cast (bind) off 5 stitches at the beginning
of the next 2 rows.
(91 (100, 109, 118, 127) stitches)
Decrease one stitch at each end of the next
and 4 following 4th rows.
(81 (90, 99, 108, 117) stitches)

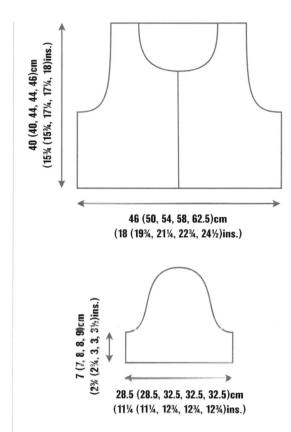

40 (40, 44, 44, 46)cm
(15¾ (15¾, 17¼, 17¼, 18)ins.)

46 (50, 54, 58, 62.5)cm
(18 (19¾, 21¼, 22¾, 24½)ins.)

7 (7, 8, 8, 9)cm
(2¾ (2¾, 3, 3, 3½)ins.)

28.5 (28.5, 32.5, 32.5, 32.5)cm
(11¼ (11¼, 12¾, 12¾, 12¾)ins.)

Continue without shaping in reverse stocking
(stockinette) stitch until armhole measures
22 (22, 24, 24, 24)cm (8¾ (8¾, 9½,
9½, 9½)ins.) from start of armhole
shaping, ending with a wrong-side row.

SHAPE SHOULDERS

Cast (bind) off 22 (27, 26, 31, 30) stitches
at the beginning of the next 2 rows.
Place the remaining 37 (36, 47, 46, 57)
stitches on a holder.

Left front

With 3.75mm (US5) needles, cast on
48 (53, 57, 62, 66) stitches.

RIB PATTERN

Row 1 (right side): K0 (3, 0, 3, 0),
p0 (2, 0, 2, 0), [k2, p2, k3, p2] to last
3 stitches, k3.

Row 2: P3, [k2, p3, k2, p2] to last
0 (5, 0, 5, 0) stitches, k0 (2, 0, 2, 0),
p0 (3, 0, 3, 0).
These 2 rows form the rib pattern.
Repeat the last 2 rows until left front
measures 5 (5, 6, 6, 7)cm (2 (2, 2¼, 2¼,
2¾)ins.) from the cast-on edge, ending with
a wrong-side row.
Change to 4mm (US6) needles.
Row 1: Purl to last 31 stitches, [k1, k2tog,
yrn, k1, yrn, k2togtbl, k1, p3] 3 times, p1.
Row 2: K1, [k3, p7] 3 times, knit to end.
Row 3: Purl to last 31 stitches, [k2tog, yrn,
k3, yrn, k2togtbl, p3] 3 times, p1.
Row 4: Repeat row 2.
Repeat the last 4 rows until the left front
measures 18 (18, 20, 20, 22)cm
(7 (7, 7¾, 7¾, 8¾)ins.) from the cast-on
edge, ending with a wrong-side row.

SHAPE ARMHOLE
Cast (bind) off 5 stitches at the beginning of
the next row. *(43 (48, 52, 57, 61) stitches)*
Work one row.
Decrease one stitch at armhole edge of next
row and 4 following 4th rows, ending with a
right-side row. *(38 (43, 47, 52, 56) stitches)*

SHAPE NECK
Next row: Work 11 (11, 15, 15, 19)
stitches in pattern, slip these stitches on a
holder, work in pattern to end.
(27 (32, 32, 37, 37) stitches)
Decrease one stitch at the neck edge of next
and every following alternate row until there
are 22 (27, 26, 31, 30) stitches.
Keeping pattern correct, continue without
shaping until armhole measures 22 (22, 24,
24, 24)cm (8¾ (8¾, 9½, 9½, 9½)ins.)
from start of armhole shaping, ending with
a wrong-side row.
Cast (bind) off.

Right front
With 3.75mm (US6) needles, cast on 48
(53, 57, 62, 66) stitches.

RIB PATTERN
Row 1 (right side): K3, [p2, k3, p2, k2] to
last 0 (5, 0, 5, 0) stitches, p0 (2, 0, 2, 0),
k0 (3, 0, 3, 0).
Row 2: P0 (3, 0, 3, 0), k0 (2, 0, 2, 0),
[p2, k2, p3, k2] to last 3 stitches, p3.
These 2 rows form the rib pattern.
Repeat the last 2 rows until right front
measures 5 (5, 6, 6, 7)cm (2 (2, 2¼, 2¼,
2¾)ins.) from the cast-on edge, ending with
a wrong-side row.
Change to 4mm (US6) needles.
Row 1: P1, [p3, k1, k2tog, yrn, k1, yrn,
k2togtbl, k1] 3 times, purl to end.
Row 2: Knit to last 31 stitches, [p7, k3]
3 times, k1.
Row 3: P1, [p3, k2tog, yrn, k3, yrn,
k2togtbl] 3 times, purl to end.
Row 4: Repeat row 2.
Repeat the last 4 rows until the right front
measures 18 (18, 20, 20, 22)cm
(7 (7, 7¾, 7¾, 8¾)ins.) from the cast-on
edge, ending with a right-side row.
Work as given for Left front, reversing
armhole and neck shapings.

Sleeves
With 3.75mm (US5) needles, cast on
63 (63, 72, 72, 72) stitches.

RIB PATTERN
Row 1 (right side): [P2, k3, p2, k2] to end.
Row 2: [P2, k2, p3, k2] to end.
These 2 rows form the rib pattern.
Repeat the last 2 rows until sleeve measures
5 (5, 6, 6, 7)cm (2 (2, 2¼, 2¼, 2¾)ins.)
from the cast-on edge, ending with a
wrong-side row.
Starting with a purl row, work 6 rows in
reverse stocking (stockinette) stitch, ending
with a wrong-side row.

SHAPE TOP
Cast (bind) off 5 stitches at the beginning of
the next 2 rows. *(53 (53, 62, 62, 62) stitches)*

hacho: short-sleeved, cropped cardigan

Decrease one stitch at each end of next and 6 following 4th rows.
(39 (39, 48, 48, 48) stitches)
Work one row.
Decrease one stitch at each end of next and 4 following alternate rows.
(29 (29, 38, 38, 38) stitches)
Work 0 (0, 1, 1, 1) row.
Decrease one stitch at each end of next and every following row until 15 (15, 18, 18, 18) stitches remain.
Cast (bind) off 5 stitches at the beginning of the next 2 rows. *(5 (5, 8, 8, 8) stitches)*
Cast (bind) off remaining stitches.

Button band left edging

With right side facing and 3.75mm (US5) needles, pick up and knit 67 (67, 71, 71, 76) stitches down left front opening edge.

RIB PATTERN

Row 1: P3, [k2, p3, k2, p2] to last 1 (1, 5, 5, 1) stitch(es), k0 (0, 2, 2,0), p1 (1, 3, 3, 1).
Row 2 (right side): K1(1, 3, 3, 1), p0 (0, 2, 2, 0), [k2, p2, k3, p2] to last 3 stitches, k3.
These 2 rows form the rib pattern.
Work 5 rows more in rib.
Cast (bind) off.

Buttonhole right edging

With right side facing and 3.75mm (US5) needles, pick up and knit 67 (67, 71, 71, 76) stitches up right front opening edge.
Starting with row 1 of rib pattern given for the Button band left edging, work 3 rows in rib.
Buttonhole row (right side): K1 (1, 3, 3, 1), p0 (0, 2, 2, 0), [k2, p2, k2tog, yrn, k1, p2] to last 3 stitches, k3.
Work 3 rows in rib.
Cast (bind) off.

Neck edging

Join shoulder seams.
With right side facing and 3.75mm (US5) needles, pick up and knit 7 stitches from edging, knit 11 (11, 15, 15, 19) stitches from holder at right front, pick up and knit 19 (20, 24, 24, 24) stitches up right front neck, knit 37 (36, 47, 46, 57) stitches from holder of the back, pick up and knit 20 (20, 24, 25, 24) stitches down left front neck, knit 11 (11, 15, 15, 19) stitches from holder at left front, pick up and knit 7 stitches from edging.
(112 (112, 139, 139, 157) stitches)

RIB PATTERN

Row 1 (wrong side): P3, [k2, p3, k2, p2] to last stitch, p1.
Row 2: K3, [p2, k3, p2, k2] to last stitch, k1
These 2 rows form the rib pattern.
Work 1 more row in rib.
Buttonhole row: K1, k2tog, yrn, work in pattern to end.
Work 3 rows in rib.
Cast (bind) off.

Finishing

Sew on sleeves, placing centre of sleeves to shoulder seams.
Join the side and sleeve seams.
Weave in ends.
Position and sew buttons into place.

QINA
three-quarter sleeve, wrap cardigan

The yarn used for this cardigan helps create the beautiful draping. In contrast, the three-quarter sleeves make the cardigan feel fitted and neat.

MEASUREMENTS

To fit bust (suggested)	81.5–86.5 32–34	91.5–96.5 36–38	101.5–106.5 40–42	106.5–112 42–44	117–122 46–48	cm ins.
Actual measurement	90 35½	100 39¼	110 43¼	120 47¼	130 51	cm ins.
Length	57 22½	57 22½	62 24½	62 24½	64 25¼	cm ins.
Sleeve length	24 9½	24 9½	24 9½	24 9½	24 9½	cm ins.

MATERIALS

10 (10, 11, 11, 12) 50g (1¾oz) hanks of
    Qina in yarn A
1 (1, 1, 1, 2) 50g (1¾oz) hanks of
    Qina in yarn B
(photographed in: yarn A, Golden Yellow,
shade 902; yarn B, Dark Navy, shade 914)

NEEDLES

One pair of 4mm (US6) knitting needles
Knitter's sewing needle or tapestry needle

TENSION (GAUGE)

20 stitches and 28 rows to 10cm (4ins.)
square over stocking (stockinette) stitch
using 4mm (US6) needles.

Please note: No edges are picked up so
please make sure all edges are neat. Join
any new balls at the side edges.

Back

With 4mm (US6) needles and yarn B, cast
on 90 (100, 110, 120, 130) stitches.
Starting with a knit row, work 5 rows in
stocking (stockinette) stitch, ending with
a right-side row.
Knit one row.
Change to yarn A.
Starting with a knit row, continue in stocking
(stockinette) stitch and yarn A only until back
measures 35 (35, 38, 38, 40)cm (13¾
(13¾, 15, 15, 15¾)ins.) from the cast-on
edge, ending with a wrong-side row.

SHAPE ARMHOLES

Cast (bind) off 4 stitches at the beginning of
the next 2 rows.
 (92, 102, 112, 122) stitches)
Decrease one stitch at each end of next and
3 following 4th rows.
(74 (84, 94, 104, 114) stitches)

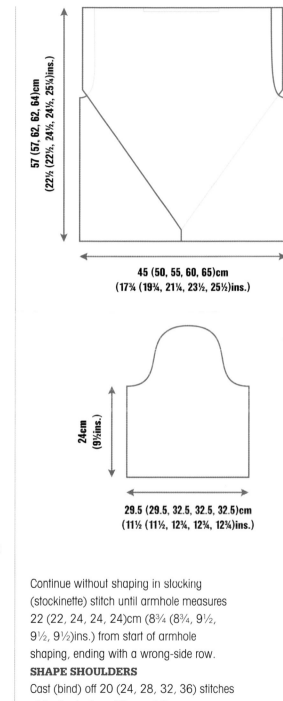

57 (57, 62, 62, 64)cm
(22½ (22½, 24½, 24½, 25¼)ins.)

45 (50, 55, 60, 65)cm
(17¾ (19¾, 21¼, 23½, 25½)ins.)

24cm
(9½ins.)

29.5 (29.5, 32.5, 32.5, 32.5)cm
(11½ (11½, 12¾, 12¾, 12¾)ins.)

Continue without shaping in stocking
(stockinette) stitch until armhole measures
22 (22, 24, 24, 24)cm (8¾ (8¾, 9½,
9½, 9½)ins.) from start of armhole
shaping, ending with a wrong-side row.

SHAPE SHOULDERS

Cast (bind) off 20 (24, 28, 32, 36) stitches
at the beginning of the next 2 rows.
Cast (bind) off the remaining 34 (36, 38,
40, 42) stitches.

Left front

With 4mm (US6) needles and yarn B, cast on 35 (45, 55, 65, 75) stitches.

Starting with a knit row, work 5 rows in stocking (stockinette) stitch, ending with a right-side row.

Knit one row.

Change to yarn A.

Row 1 (right side): Knit to end.

Row 2: Knit to last 20 (24, 28, 32, 36) stitches, purl to end.

These 2 rows set the position of the stocking (stockinette) stitch and garter stitch at the front opening edge.

Keeping the stocking (stockinette) stitch over the 20 (24, 28, 32, 36) stitches, increase as follows, taking the increase stitches into the garter stitch.

Increase row (right side): Knit to last 3 stitches, m1, k3.

Increase one stitch at front edge as set above on every following alternate row, until left front measures 35 (35, 38, 38, 40)cm (13¾ (13¾, 15, 15, 15¾)ins.) from the cast-on edge, ending with a wrong-side row.

Continue to increase one stitch at neck edge at the same time shape armhole as follows:

SHAPE ARMHOLE

Cast (bind) off 4 stitches at the beginning of the next row.

Work one row.

Decrease one stitch at armhole edge of next and 3 following 4th rows.

Continue to increase one stitch at neck edge as before until there are 82 (92, 102, 112, 122) stitches, ending with a right-side row.

Continue without shaping until armhole measures 22 (22, 24, 24, 24)cm (8¾ (8¾, 9½, 9½, 9½)ins.) from start of armhole shaping, ending with a right-side row.

Next row: Cast (bind) off 62 (68, 74, 80, 86) stitches, work in pattern to end.

Cast (bind) off remaining 20 (24, 28, 32, 36) stitches.

Right front

With 4mm (US6) needles and yarn B, cast on 35 (45, 55, 65, 75) stitches.

Starting with a knit row, work 5 rows in stocking (stockinette) stitch, ending with a right-side row.

Knit one row.

Change to yarn A.

Row 1 (right side): Knit to end.

Row 2: Purl 20 (24, 28, 32, 36) stitches, knit to end.

These 2 rows set the position of the stocking (stockinette) stitch and garter stitch at the front opening edge.

Keeping the stocking (stockinette) stitch over the 20 (24, 28, 32, 36) stitches, increase as follows, taking the increase stitches into the garter stitch.

Increase row (right side): K3, m1, knit to end.

Work as given for Left front, reversing shapings.

Sleeves

With 4mm (US6) needles and yarn B, cast on 59 (59, 65, 65, 65) stitches.

Starting with a knit row, work 5 rows in stocking (stockinette) stitch, ending with a right-side row.

Knit one row.

Change to yarn A.

Starting with a knit row, continue in stocking (stockinette) stitch until sleeve measures 24cm (9½ins.) from the cast-on edge, ending with a wrong-side row.

SHAPE TOP

Cast (bind) off 4 stitches at the beginning of the next 2 rows.

(51 (51, 57, 57, 57) stitches)

Decrease one stitch at each end of next and 5 following 4th rows.

(39 (39, 45, 45, 45) stitches)

Work one row.

Decrease one stitch at each end of next and 4 following alternate rows.
(29 (29, 35, 35, 35) stitches)
Work 3 rows.
Decrease one stitch at each end of next and every following row until 17 (17, 21, 21, 21) stitches remain.
Cast (bind) off 5 stitches at the beginning of the next 2 rows. *(7 (7, 11, 11, 11) stitches)*
Cast (bind) off remaining stitches.

Finishing

Join shoulder seams.
Sew on sleeves, placing centre of sleeves to shoulder seams.
Weave in ends.
Join the side and sleeve seams.

SULKA

high collar, short-sleeved cardigan

The stitches used to create this cardigan create the fitted look without any other fitted shaping. It is the subtle details that create an amazing garment and on a cardigan the buttons are particularly important. A contrasting button can create an exciting and completely different look.

MEASUREMENTS

To fit bust	76.5–81.5	81.5–86.5	91.5–96.5	96.5–101.5	106.5–112	cm
(suggested)	30–32	32–34	36–38	38–40	42–44	ins.
Actual	81.5	90	98.5	107	115.5	cm
measurement	32	35½	38¾	42¼	45½	ins.
Length	60	60	62	66	66	cm
	23½	23½	24½	26	26	ins.
Sleeve length	6	6	6	6	6	cm
	2¼	2¼	2¼	2¼	2¼	ins.

MATERIALS

12 (12, 13, 14, 15) 50g (1¾oz) hanks of
    Sulka
(photographed in Paprika, shade 208)

11 medium-sized buttons

NEEDLES

One pair of 5mm (US8) knitting needles
One pair of 6mm (US10) knitting needles
Five stitch holders
Knitter's sewing needle or tapestry needle

TENSION (GAUGE)

14 stitches and 21 rows to 10cm (4ins.)
square over stocking (stockinette) stitch
using 6mm (US10) needles.

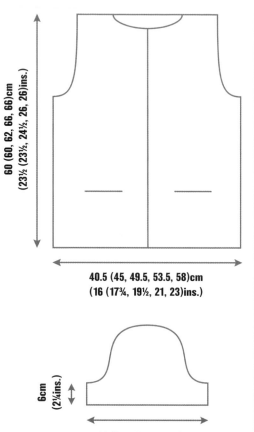

60 (60, 62, 66, 66)cm (23½ (23½, 24½, 26, 26)ins.)

40.5 (45, 49.5, 53.5, 58)cm (16 (17¾, 19½, 21, 23)ins.)

6cm (2¼ins.)

28 (28, 32, 32, 36.5)cm (11 (11, 12½, 12½, 14¼)ins.)

Back

With 6mm (US10) needles, cast on 57 (63, 69, 75, 81) stitches.

RIB PATTERN

Row 1 (right side): K3, [p3, k3] to end.
Row 2: P3, [k3, p3] to end.
These 2 rows form the rib pattern.
Repeat the last 2 rows until rib measures 15cm (6ins.) from the cast-on edge, ending with a wrong-side row.
Starting with a knit row, continue in stocking (stockinette) stitch until the back measures 38 (38, 40, 42, 42)cm (15 (15, 15¾, 16½, 16½)ins.) from the cast-on edge, ending with a wrong-side row.

SHAPE ARMHOLES

Cast (bind) off 4 stitches at the beginning of the next 2 rows.
(49 (55, 61, 67, 73) stitches)
Decrease one stitch at each end of next and 3 following 4th rows.
(41 (47, 53, 59, 65) stitches)
Continue without shaping in stocking (stockinette) stitch until armhole measures 22 (22, 22, 24, 24)cm (8¾ (8¾, 8¾, 9½, 9½)ins.) from start of armhole shaping, ending with a wrong-side row.

SHAPE SHOULDERS

Cast (bind) off 10 (12, 14, 16, 18) stitches at the beginning of the next 2 rows.
Place the remaining 21 (23, 25, 27, 29) stitches on a holder.

Pocket linings (make two)

With 6mm (US10) needles, cast on 15 (15, 15, 21, 21) stitches.
Starting with a row 1 of Back rib pattern, continue in rib pattern until pocket lining measures 15cm (6ins.) from the cast-on edge, ending with a wrong-side row.
Place the remaining stitches on a holder.

Left front

With 6mm (US10) needles, cast on 28 (31, 34, 37, 40) stitches.

RIB PATTERN

Row 1 (right side): P0 (3, 0, 3, 0), [k3, p3] to last 4 stitches, k4.
Row 2: P4, [k3, p3] to last 0 (3, 0, 3, 0) stitches, k0 (3, 0, 3, 0).
These 2 rows form the rib pattern.
Repeat the last 2 rows until rib measures 15cm (6ins.) from the cast-on edge, ending with a wrong-side row.
Pocket placement row: K6 (9, 12, 9, 12) stitches, place next 15 (15, 15, 21, 21) stitches onto a holder, k15 (15, 15, 21, 21)

stitches along one pocket lining, knit to end.
Purl one row.

Starting with a knit row, continue in stocking (stockinette) stitch until the left front measures 38 (38, 40, 42, 42)cm (15 (15, 15¾, 16½, 16½)ins.) from the cast-on edge, ending with a wrong-side row.

SHAPE ARMHOLE

Cast (bind) off 4 stitches at the beginning of the next row. *(24 (27, 30, 33, 36) stitches)*
Purl one row.
Decrease one stitch at armhole edge of next row and 3 following 4th rows.
(20 (23, 26, 29, 32) stitches)
Continue without shaping in stocking (stockinette) stitch until armhole measures 18 (18, 18, 20, 20)cm (7 (7, 7, 7¾, 7¾)ins.) from start of armhole shaping, ending with a right-side row.

SHAPE NECK

Next row: P6 (7, 8, 9, 10) stitches, slip these stitches on a holder, purl to end.
(14 (16, 18, 20, 22) stitches)
Decrease one stitch at the neck edge of next row and then every row until there are 10 (12, 14, 16, 18) stitches.
Continue without shaping in stocking (stockinette) stitch until armhole measures 22 (22, 22, 24, 24)cm (8¾ (8¾, 8¾, 9½, 9½)ins. from start of armhole shaping, ending with a wrong-side row.
Cast (bind) off.

Right front

With 6mm (US10) needles, cast on 28 (31, 34, 37, 40) stitches.

RIB PATTERN

Row 1 (right side): K4, [p3, k3] to last 0 (3, 0, 3, 0) stitches, p0 (3, 0, 3, 0).
Row 2: K0 (3, 0, 3, 0), [p3, k3] to last 4 stitches, p4.
These 2 rows form the rib pattern.
Repeat the last 2 rows until rib measures

15cm (6ins.) from the cast-on edge, ending with a wrong-side row.

Pocket placement row: K7, place next 15 (15, 15, 21, 21) stitches onto a holder, k15 (15, 15, 21, 21) stitches along one pocket lining, knit to end.

Purl one row.

Complete as given for Left front, but reversing shapings.

Sleeves

With 6mm (US10) needles, cast on 39 (39, 45, 45, 51) stitches.

Starting with a row 1 of Back rib pattern, continue in rib pattern until sleeve measures 5cm (2ins.) from the cast-on edge, ending with a wrong-side row.

Starting with knit row, continue in stocking (stockinette) stitch until sleeve measures 6cm (2¼ins.) from the cast-on edge, ending with a wrong-side row.

SHAPE TOP

Cast (bind) off 4 stitches at the beginning of the next 2 rows.

(31 (31, 37, 37, 43) stitches)

Decrease one stitch at each end of next and 4 following 4th rows.

(21 (21, 27, 27, 33) stitches)

Purl one row.

Decrease one stitch at each end of next row and every 3 following alternate rows.

(13 (13, 19, 19, 25) stitches)

Decrease one stitch at each end of next and every following row until 7 (7, 9, 9, 15) stitches remain.

Cast (bind) off 3 (3, 4, 4, 7) stitches at the beginning of the next 2 rows. *(1 stitch)*

Cast (bind) off remaining stitch.

Collar

Join shoulder seams.

With right side facing and 5mm (US8) needles, knit 6 (7, 8, 9, 10) stitches from holder at right front, pick up and knit 10 (11, 9, 10, 11) stitches up right front neck, knit 21 (23, 25, 27, 29) stitches from holder for the back, pick up and knit 10 (11, 9, 10, 11) stitches along left front neck, knit 6 (7, 8, 9, 10) stitches from holder at left front. *(53 (59, 59, 65, 71) stitches)*

RIB PATTERN

Row 1 (wrong side): P4, [k3, p3] to last stitch, p1.

Row 2: K4, [p3, k3] to last stitch, k1.

Repeat the last 2 rows until collar measures 10cm (4ins.), ending with a right-side row.

Next row (right side): K4, [p3, k3] to last stitch, k1.

Next row: P4, [k3, p3] to last stitch, p1.

Repeat the last 2 rows until collar measures 22cm (8¾ins.), ending with a wrong-side row.

Cast (bind) off.

Left edging

With right side facing and 5mm (US8) needles, measure 12cm (4¾ins.) down from top of collar, pick up and knit 17 stitches up left collar from this point, break yarn, slip these stitches onto needle, with same needle then pick up and knit 15 stitches down left edge of collar and pick up and knit 81 (81, 84, 87, 87) stitches down left edge.

(113 (113, 116, 119, 119) stitches)

RIB PATTERN

Row 1: P4 (4, 1, 4, 4), *k3, p3, repeat from * to last 19 stitches, [p3, k3] to last stitch, k1.

Row 2: P4, [k3, p3] twice, k3, *k3, p3, repeat from * to last 4 (4, 1, 4, 4) stitches, knit to end.

Work the rib row 1 again.

Buttonhole row: P4, cast (bind) off 3 stitches, work in the pattern to end.

Next row: Work in the pattern, casting on 3 stitches over those cast (bound) off on previous row.

Work 3 more rows in rib pattern.

Cast (bind) off.

Right edging

With right side facing and 5mm (US8) needles, pick up and knit 81 (81, 84, 87, 87) stitches up right front opening edge and pick up and knit 15 stitches up right edge of collar to same point as on left edge, break yarn, with another needle then pick up and knit 17 stitches down right edge of collar, break yarn and slip these stitches onto the needle with the other stitches.

113 (113, 116, 119, 119) stitches)

Rejoin yarn with wrong-side facing.

RIB PATTERN

Row 1: K1 [k3, p3] 3 times, *p3, k3, repeat from * to last 4 (4, 1, 4, 4) stitches, p4 (4, 1, 4, 4).

Row 2: K4, (4, 1, 4, 4,), *p3, k3, repeat from * to the last 19 stitches, [k3, p3] 3 times, p1.

Work the rib row 1 again.

Buttonhole row: K4, cast (bind) off 3 stitches, [rib 9 stitches, cast (bind) off 3 stitches] 4 times, work in pattern to end.

Next row: Work in pattern to end, casting on 3 stitches over those cast (bound) off on previous row.

Work 3 more rows in rib pattern.

Cast (bind) off.

Pocket tops

With right side facing and 6mm (US10) needles, work in pattern 15 (15, 15, 21, 21) stitches from pocket top holder.

RIB PATTERN

Row 1: P3, [k3, p3] to end.

Row 2 (right side). K3, [p3, k3] to end.

Buttonhole row: Work in pattern for 6 (6, 6, 9, 9) stitches, cast (bind) off 3 stitches, work in pattern to end.

Next row: Work in pattern, casting on 3 stitches over those cast (bound) off on previous row.

Work 3 rows in rib.

Cast (bind) off.

Finishing

Sew on sleeves, placing centre of sleeves to shoulder seams.

Join the side and sleeve seams.

Position and sew buttons into place.

Sew pocket linings in place on wrong side.

Catch down sides of pocket tops.

Weave in ends.

QINA
long, ribbed, v-neck cardigan

A long, ribbed, v-neck cardigan is so practical and easy to wear. To make your cardigan unique, experiment with the shades to match others in your wardrobe.

MEASUREMENTS

To fit bust	81.5–86.5	91.5–96.5	96.5–101.5	106.5–112	112–117	cm
(suggested)	32–34	36–38	38–40	42–44	44–46	ins.
Actual	97	103	109	115	121	cm
measurement	38	40½	43	45¼	47½	ins.
Length	68	70	72	74	74	cm
	26¾	27½	28¼	29¼	29¼	ins.
Sleeve length	45	45	45	45	45	cm
	17¾	17¾	17¾	17¾	17¾	ins.

MATERIALS

12 (13, 13, 14, 14) 50g (1¾oz) hanks of
Qina in yarn A

One 50g (1¾oz) hank of Qina in yarn B and
yarn D

1 (1, 2, 2, 2) 50g (1¾oz) hank(s) of Qina
in yarn C

(photographed in: yarn A, Slate Grey, shade
shade 915; yarn B, Golden Yellow, shade
902; yarn C, Charcoal Black, shade 909;
yarn D, Steel, shade 901)

3 poppers

NEEDLES

One long 3.75mm (US5) circular needle
One pair of 3.75mm (US5) knitting needles
One pair of 4mm (US6) knitting needles
Four stitch holders
Knitter's sewing needle or tapestry needle

TENSION (GAUGE)

20 stitches and 28 rows to 10cm (4ins.)
square over main pattern using 4mm
(US6) needles.

Back

With 4mm (US6) needles with yarn B, cast
on 97 (103, 109, 115, 121) stitches.

RIB PATTERN

Row 1 (right side): Knit to end.
Change to yarn C.
Row 2: P1, [p2, k1] to last 3 stitches, p3.
These 2 rows form the rib stitch pattern.
Work a further 4 rows in rib stitch in
yarn C only.
Change to yarn D.
Repeat rib row 1.
Working with yarn A only:

MAIN PATTERN

Row 1 (wrong side): P3, k1, [p5, k1] to
last 3 stitches, p3.
Row 2 (right side): Knit to end.

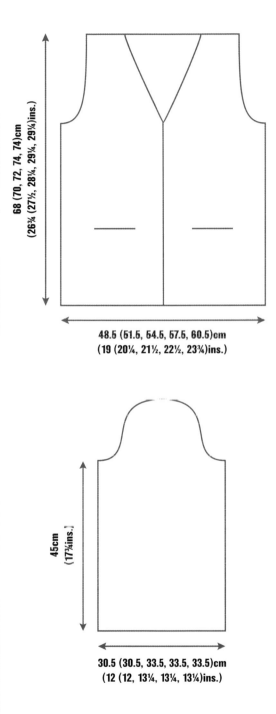

68 (70, 72, 74, 74)cm
(26¾ (27½, 28½, 29¼, 29¼)ins.)

48.5 (51.5, 54.5, 57.5, 60.5)cm
(19 (20¼, 21½, 22½, 23¾)ins.)

45cm
(17¾ins.)

30.5 (30.5, 33.5, 33.5, 33.5)cm
(12 (12, 13¼, 13¼, 13¼)ins.)

These 2 rows form the main stitch pattern. Repeat the last 2 rows until back measures 46 (48, 48, 50, 50)cm (18 (18¾, 18¾, 19¾, 19¾)ins.) from the cast-on edge, ending with a wrong-side row.

SHAPE ARMHOLES

Cast (bind) off 5 stitches at the beginning of the next 2 rows.

(87 (93, 99, 105, 111) stitches)

Decrease one stitch at each end of next and 4 following 4th rows.

(77 (83, 89, 95, 101) stitches)

Continue without shaping in the main stitch pattern until armhole measures 22 (22, 24, 24, 24)cm (8¾ (8¾, 9½, 9½, 9½)ins.) from start of armhole shaping, ending with a wrong-side row.

SHAPE SHOULDERS

Cast (bind) off 21 (23, 25, 27, 29) stitches at the beginning of next 2 rows.

Place the remaining 35 (37, 39, 41, 43) stitches on a holder.

Pocket linings (make two)

With 4mm (US6) needles and yarn A, cast on 25 (25, 31, 31, 37) stitches.

Starting with a row 2 of the main stitch pattern as given for the back, work as given for the back until pocket lining measures 15 (17, 17, 19, 19)cm (6 (6½, 6½, 7½, 7½)ins.) from the cast-on edge, ending with a wrong-side row.

Place the stitches on a holder.

Left front

With 4mm (US6) needles and yarn B, cast on 46 (49, 52, 55, 58) stitches.

RIB PATTERN

Row 1 (right side): Knit to end.

Change to yarn C.

Row 2: P1, [p2, k1] to last 3 stitches, p3.

These 2 rows form the rib stitch pattern.

Work a further 4 rows in rib stitch in yarn C only.

Change to yarn D.

Repeat rib row 1.

Working with yarn A only:

MAIN STITCH PATTERN

Row 1 (wrong side): P0 (3, 0, 3, 0), k1, [p5, k1] to last 3 stitches, p3.

Row 2 (right side): Knit to end.

These 2 rows form the main stitch pattern. Repeat the last 2 rows until left front measures 18 (20, 20, 22, 22)cm (7 (7¾, 7¾, 8¾, 8¾)ins.) from the cast-on edge, ending with a wrong-side row.

Pocket placement row: Knit 12 stitches, place next 25 (25, 31, 31, 37) stitches onto a holder, knit 25 (25, 31, 31, 37) stitches along one pocket lining, knit to end.

Continue in main stitch pattern until left front measures 46 (48, 48, 50, 50)cm (18 (18¾, 18¾, 19¾, 19¾)ins.) from the cast-on edge, ending with a wrong-side row.

SHAPE ARMHOLE AND NECK

Cast (bind) off 5 stitches at the beginning of the next row. *(41 (44, 47, 50, 53) stitches)* Work one row.

Decrease one stitch at armhole edge of next and 4 following 4th rows at the same time decrease one stitch at neck edge of next and following 2 (4, 3, 5, 7) alternate rows and then, on every following 4th row until there are 21 (23, 25, 28, 29) stitches.

Continue without shaping in main stitch pattern until armhole measures 22 (22, 24, 24, 24)cm (8¾ (8¾, 9½, 9½, 9½)ins.) from start of armhole shaping, ending with a wrong-side row.

Cast (bind) off.

Right front

With 4mm (US6) needles and yarn B, cast on 46 (49, 52, 55, 58) stitches.

RIB PATTERN

Row 1 (right side): Knit to end.

Change to yarn C.

Row 2: P1, [p2, k1] to last 3 stitches, p3.

These 2 rows form the rib stitch pattern.

Work a further 4 rows in rib stitch in yarn C only.

Change to yarn D.

Repeat rib row 1.

Working with yarn A only.

MAIN PATTERN

Row 1 (wrong side): P3, [k1, p5] to last 1 (4, 1, 4, 1) stitches, k1, p0 (3, 0, 3, 0).

Row 2 (right side): Knit to end.

Repeat the last 2 rows until right front measures 18 (20, 20, 22, 22)cm (7 (7¾, 7¾, 8¾, 8¾)ins.) from the cast-on edge, ending with a wrong-side row.

Pocket placement row: Knit 9 (12, 9, 12, 9) stitches, place next 25 (25, 31, 31, 37) stitches onto a holder, knit 25 (25, 31, 31, 37) stitches along one pocket lining, knit to end.

Continue in main stitch pattern until right front measures 46 (48, 48, 50, 50)cm (18 (18¾, 18¾, 19¾, 9¾)ins.) from the cast-on edge, ending with a right-side row. Work as given for Left front, reversing shape armhole and neck.

Sleeves

With 4mm (US6) needles and yarn B, cast on 61 (61, 67, 67, 67) stitches.

Work as given for the back until sleeve measures 45cm (17¾ins.) from the cast-on edge, ending with a wrong-side row.

SHAPE TOP

Cast (bind) off 5 stitches at the beginning of the next 2 rows. *(51 (51, 57, 57, 57) stitches)*

Decrease one stitch at each end of next and 7 following 4th rows.

(35 (35, 41, 41, 41) stitches)

Work one row.

Decrease one stitch at each end of next and 6 following alternate rows.

(21 (21, 27, 27, 27) stitches)

Work one row.

Decrease one stitch at each end of next and every following row until 9 (9, 11, 11, 11) stitches remain.

Cast (bind) off remaining stitches.

Pocket tops

With right side facing, 3.75mm (US5) needles and yarn D, pick up and knit 25 (25, 31, 31, 37) stitches from pocket top holder.

With yarn C, work 5 rows in main pattern.

With yarn B, knit one row.

Cast (bind) off in pattern with yarn B on wrong-side row.

Edging

Join shoulder seams.

With right side facing, using a long 3.75mm (US5) circular needle and yarn B, pick up and knit 2 stitches, with yarn C, pick up and knit 4 stitches, with yarn D, pick up and knit one stitch, with yarn A pick up and knit 120 (123, 127, 129, 129) stitches up right front opening edge, knit 35 (37, 39, 41, 43) stitches from holder at back neck, pick up and knit 120 (124, 127, 129, 130) stitches down left front opening edge, with yarn D pick up and knit one stitch, with yarn C pick up and knit 4 stitches, with yarn B pick up and knit 2 stitches. *(289 (298, 307, 313, 316) stitches)*

Row 1 (wrong side): With yarn B, p2, with yarn C, p1, k1, p2, with yarn D, k1, with yarn A, p2 [p2, k1] to last 9 stitches, with yarn D, k1, with yarn C, p2, k1, p1, with yarn B, p2.

Row 2: With yarn B, k2, with yarn C, k4, with yarn D, k1, with yarn A, knit to last 7 stitches, with yarn D, k1, with yarn C, k4, with yarn B, k2.

Repeat the row 1 once more.

Row 4: With yarn B, k2, with yarn C, k4, with yarn D, knit until the last 6 stitches, with yarn C, k4, with yarn B, k2.

Row 5: With yarn B, p2, with yarn C, p1, k1, [p2, k1] to last 3 stitches, with yarn C, p1, with yarn B, p2.

Row 6: With yarn B, k2, with yarn C, knit until the last 2 stitches, with yarn B, k2.

Repeat the last 2 rows once more.

Repeat row 5 again.

Row 10: With yarn B, p1, [p2, k1] to last 3 stitches, p3.

With yarn B, cast (bind) off knitwise.

Finishing

Sew on sleeves, placing centre of sleeves to shoulder seams.

Join the side and sleeve seams.

Position and sew poppers into place.

Sew pocket linings in place on wrong side.

Catch down sides of pocket tops.

Weave in ends.

TUPA
cropped, v-neck cardigan

This cardigan plays with one of my favourite techniques – the slip stitch. This technique creates a fabric that looks complicated but is actually really easy to do – the best type of knitting! Even subtle shade changes can transform the whole look of the cardigan.

MEASUREMENTS

To fit bust (suggested)					
81.5–86.5	86.5–91.5	91.5–96.5	101.5–106.5	106.5–112	cm
32–34	34–36	36–38	40–42	42–44	ins.
Actual measurement					
90	94.5	101	108.5	117.5	cm
35½	37¼	39¼	42¾	46¼	ins
Length					
44	44	48	50	52	cm
17¼	17¼	19	19¾	20½	ins.
Sleeve length					
22	22	22	24	24	cm
8¾	8¾	8¾	9½	9½	ins.

MATERIALS

3 (3, 4, 4, 5) 50g (1¾oz) hanks of
 Tupa in yarn A
6 (6, 6, 7, 7) 50g (1¾oz) hanks of
 Tupa in yarn B
(photographed in: yarn A, Sapphire, shade
809; yarn B, Viridian, shade 804)

3 small buttons

NEEDLES

One long 3.75mm (US5) circular
 knitting needle
One pair of 3.75mm (US5) knitting needles
One pair of 4mm (US6) knitting needles
One stitch holder
Knitter's sewing needle or tapestry needle

TENSION (GAUGE)

26 stitches and 48 rows to 10cm (4ins.) square over pattern using 4mm (US6) needles.

Note: When slipping the stitch on a wrong-side row bring the yarn forward so that it is on the wrong side when slipping, then take it back to knit the next stitch.

Back

With 3.75mm (US5) needles and yarn B, cast on 350 (368, 392, 422, 458) stitches.

EDGING FRILL

Decrease row 1 (right side): [K2tog] to end. *(175 (184, 196, 211, 229) stitches)*

Decrease row 2: P1, [p2tog, p1] to end. *(117 (123, 131, 141, 153) stitches)*

RIB PATTERN

Row 1: K1, [p1, k1] to end.

Row 2: P1, [k1, p1] to end.

These 2 rows form the rib pattern.

Repeat the last 2 rows until back measures 10cm (4ins.) from the cast-on edge, ending with a wrong-side row.

Change to 4mm (US6) needles.

SLIP STITCH PATTERN

Row 1: With yarn A, k1, [sl1, k1] to end.

Row 2: With yarn A, sl1, [k1, s l] to end.

Row 3: With yarn B, repeat row 1.

Row 4: With yarn B, repeat row 2.

These 4 rows form the slip stitch pattern.

Repeat the last 4 rows until back measures 22 (22, 24, 26, 28)cm (8¾ (8¾, 9½, 10¼, 11)ins.) from the cast-on edge, ending with a wrong-side row.

SHAPE ARMHOLES

Cast (bind) off 5 stitches at the beginning of the next 2 rows.

(107 (113, 121, 131, 143) stitches)

Decrease one stitch at each end of next and 4 following 4th rows.

(97 (103, 111, 121, 133) stitches)

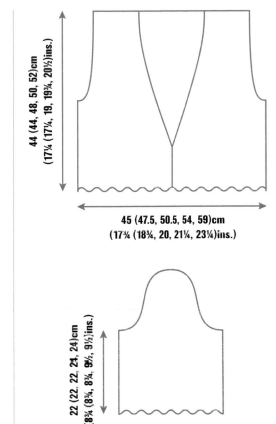

44 (44, 48, 50, 52)cm
(17¼ (17¼, 19, 19¾, 20½)ins.)

45 (47.5, 50.5, 54, 59)cm
(17¾ (18¾, 20, 21¼, 23¼)ins.)

22 (22, 22, 24, 24)cm
(8¾ (8¾, 8¾, 9½, 9½)ins.)

30.5 (30.5, 32.5, 32.5, 32.5)cm
(12 (12, 12¾, 12¾, 12¾)ins.)

Continue without shaping in pattern until armhole measures 22 (22, 24, 24, 24)cm (8¾ (8¾, 9½, 9½, 9½)ins.) from start of armhole shaping, ending with a wrong-side row.

SHAPE SHOULDERS

Cast (bind) off 27 (29, 33, 37, 41) stitches at the beginning of the next 2 rows.

Place the remaining 43 (45, 45, 47, 51) stitches on a holder.

Left front

With 3.75mm (US5) needles and yarn B, cast on 176 (182, 194, 212, 230) stitches.

EDGING FRILL

Decrease row 1 (right side): [K2tog] to end. *(88 (91, 97, 106, 115) stitches)*

Decrease row 2: P1, [p2tog, p1] to end. *(59 (61, 65, 71, 77) stitches)*

Starting with Back rib row 1, work in rib pattern until left front measures 10cm (4ins.) from the cast-on edge, ending with a wrong-side row.

Change to 4mm (US6) needles.

Starting with Back slip stitch pattern 1, work 4 rows in slip stitch pattern.

Continue to work slip stitch pattern and work neck shaping as follows:

SHAPE NECK

Next row: Work in pattern to last 5 stitches, k2tog, work 3 stitches in pattern.

Work 3 rows in pattern.

Keeping pattern correct, decrease one stitch as set at neck edge on next and every 4th row until left front measures 22 (22, 24, 26, 28)cm (8¾ (8¾, 9½, 10¼, 11)ins.) from the cast-on edge, ending with a wrong-side row and 3 rows straight since last decrease.

SHAPE ARMHOLE AND NECK

Next row: Cast (bind) off 5 stitches, work in the pattern to last 5 stitches, k2tog, work 3 stitches in pattern.

Work one row in pattern.

Decrease one stitch at armhole edge of next and 4 following 4th rows at the same time continue to decrease one stitch at neck edge on every 4th row until 27 (29, 33, 37, 41) stitches remain.

Continue without shaping in pattern until armhole measures 22 (22, 24, 24, 24)cm (8¾ (8¾, 9½, 9½, 9½)ins.) from start of armhole shaping, ending with a wrong-side row.

Cast (bind) off.

Right front

With 3.75mm (US5) needles, cast on 176 (182, 194, 212, 230) stitches.

Starting with Edging frill decrease row 1, work as given for the Left front until shape neck.

SHAPE NECK

Next row: K3, s1 knitwise, k1, psso, pattern to end.

Work as for Left front, reversing shapings.

Sleeves

With 3.75mm (US5) needles and yarn B, cast on 236 (236, 254, 254, 254) stitches.

EDGING FRILL

Decrease row 1 (right side): [K2tog] to end. *(118 (118, 127, 127, 127) stitches)*

Decrease row 2: P1, [p2tog, p1] to end. *(79 (79, 85, 85, 85) stitches)*

Starting with Back rib row 1, work in rib pattern until left front measures 5cm (2ins.) from the cast-on edge, ending with a wrong-side row.

Change to 4mm (US6) needles.

Starting with Back slip stitch pattern row 1, work until sleeve measures 22 (22, 22, 24, 24)cm (8¾ (8¾, 8¾, 9½, 9½)ins.) from the cast-on edge, ending with a wrong-side row.

SHAPE TOP

Cast (bind) off 5 stitches at the beginning of the next 2 rows.

(69 (69, 75, 75, 75) stitches)

Decrease one stitch at each end of next and 8 following 4th rows.

(51 (51, 57, 57, 57) stitches)

Work one row in pattern.

Decrease one stitch at each end of next and 5 following alternate rows.

(39 (39, 45, 45, 45) stitches)

Work one row in pattern.

Decrease one stitch at each end of next and every following row until 15 (15, 19, 19, 19) stitches remain.

Cast (bind) off.

Neck edging

Join shoulder seams.

With right side facing, yarn B and long circular 3.75mm (US5) needle, pick up and knit 90 (90, 95, 100, 105) stitches up right front edging from top of frill, knit 43 (45, 45, 47, 51) stitches from holder at centre back, pick up and knit 90 (90, 95, 100, 105) stitches down left front edging to top of frill. *(223 (225, 235, 247, 261) stitches)*

Next row: Knit to last 16 stitches, k2tog, yrn, [k4, yrn, k2tog] to last 2 stitches, k2. Knit one row.

Cast (bind) off on wrong-side row.

Finishing

Sew on sleeves, placing centre of sleeves to shoulder seams.

Join the side and sleeve seams.

Position and sew buttons into place.

Weave in ends.

SULKA
edge-to-edge lace and cable, chunky jacket

This jacket plays with traditional ideas and uses a solid chunky yarn to create a delicate lace pattern next to a structured cable pattern. The rolled edgings seem to let the knitting free and do what it does naturally.

MEASUREMENTS

To fit bust	81.5–91.5	96.5–106.5	112–132	cm
(suggested)	32–36	38–42	44–52	ins.
Actual	92	118.5	145	cm
measurement	36¼	46½	57¼	ins.
Length	62	67	72	cm
	24½	26¼	28¼	ins.
Sleeve length	40	40	42	cm
	15¾	15¾	16½	ins.

MATERIALS

18 (20, 22) 50g (1¾oz) hanks of Sulka
(photographed in Denim Blue, shade 221)

One decorative clasp

NEEDLES

One pair of 5mm (US8) knitting needles
One pair of 6mm (US10) knitting needles
One cable needle
Three stitch holders
Knitter's sewing needle or tapestry needle

TENSION (GAUGE)

15 stitches and 18 rows to 10cm (4ins.)
square over lace pattern using 6mm (US10)
needles.

SPECIAL ABBREVIATIONS

C2B: Slip next stitch onto cable needle and
hold at back, k1 from left-hand needle, k1
from cable needle.

C4B: Slip next 2 stitches onto cable needle
and hold at back, k2 from left-hand needle,
k2 from cable needle.

C4F: Slip next 2 stitches onto cable needle
and hold at front, k2 from left-hand needle,
k2 from cable needle.

T2B: Slip next stitch onto cable needle and
hold at back, k1 from left-hand needle, p1
from cable needle.

T2F: Slip next stitch onto cable needle and
hold at front, p1 from left-hand needle, k1
from cable needle.

T4B: Slip next 2 stitches onto cable needle
and hold at back, k2 from left-hand needle,
p2 from cable needle.

T4F: Slip next 2 stitches onto cable needle
and hold at front, p2 from left-hand needle,
k2 from cable needle.

Back and fronts

(knitted in one piece up to armholes)
With 6mm (US10) needles, cast on 159
(199, 239) stitches.
Knit 2 rows.

MAIN STITCH PATTERN

Row 1 (right side): K2, p4, T4F, p1, C2B,
p1, T4B, p4, k3, [yrn, k3, sl1, k2tog, psso,
k3, yrn, k1] to last 24 stitches, k2, p4, T4F,
p1, C2B, p1, T4B, p4, k2.

Row 2: P2, k6, [p2, k1] twice, p2, k6, p2,
purl to last 24 stitches, p2, k6, [p2, k1]
twice, p2, k6, p2.

Row 3: T4F, p4, T4F, T4B, p4, T4B, p1,
[k1, yrn, k2, sl1, k2tog, psso, k2, yrn, k1,
p1] to last 24 stitches, T4F, p4, T4F, T4B,
p4, T4B.

Row 4: K2, p2, k6, p4, k6, p2, k3, [p9, k1]
to last 24 stitches, k2, p2, k6, p4, k6,
p2, k2.

Row 5: P2, C4F, p4, T2F, T2B, p4, C4B,
p3, [k2, yrn, k1, sl1, k2tog, psso, k1, yrn,
k2, p1] to last 24 stitches, p2, C4F, p4,
T2F, T2B, p4, C4B, p2.

Row 6: K2, p4, k5, p2, k5, p4, k3, [p9, k1]
to last 24 stitches, k2, p4, k5, p2, k5,
p4, k2.

Row 7: T4B, T4F, p3, C2B, p3, T4B, T4F,
p1, [k3, yrn, sl1, k2tog, psso, yrn, k3, p1]
to last 24 stitches, T4B, T4F, p3, C2B, p3,
T4B, T4F.

Row 8: P2, k4, [p2, k3] twice, p2, k4, p2,
purl to last 24 stitches, p2, k4, [p2, k3]
twice, p2, k4, p2.

These 8 rows form the main stitch pattern.
Repeat the last 8 rows until work measures
42 (44, 45)cm (16½ (17½, 17¾)ins.)
from the cast-on edge, ending with
a wrong-side row.
Divide for fronts.

RIGHT FRONT

Next row: Work in pattern until there are 45
(55, 65) stitches on right hand needle, turn,
place the remaining stitches on a holder.

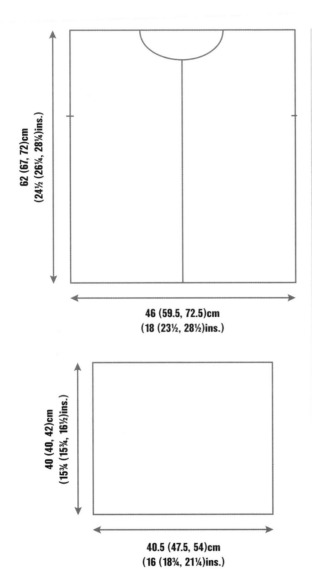

62 (67, 72)cm
(24½ (26¼, 28¼)ins.)

46 (59.5, 72.5)cm
(18 (23½, 28½)ins.)

40 (40, 42)cm
(15¾ (15¾, 16½)ins.)

40.5 (47.5, 54)cm
(16 (18¾, 21¼)ins.)

Keeping pattern correct, continue to work on these 45 (55, 65) stitches until work measures 54 (59, 64)cm (21¼ (23¼, 25)ins.) from the cast-on edge, ending with a wrong-side row.

SHAPE NECK

Next row: Work 11 (16, 21) stitches in pattern, place these 11 (16, 21) stitches on a holder, work in pattern to end.
(34 (39, 44) stitches)
Work one row in pattern.
Decrease one stitch at neck edge on next and every following row until there are 24 (29, 34) stitches.
Continue in pattern without shaping until work measures 62 (67, 72)cm (24½ (26¼, 28¼)ins.) from the cast-on edge, ending with a wrong-side row.
Cast (bind) off.

BACK

With right side facing, rejoin yarn to centre 69 (89, 09) stitches, increasing one stitch at each end of row. *(71 (91, 111) stitches)*
Keeping pattern correct with first and last stitch as knit on right side and purl on wrong side, continue in pattern until work measures 62 (67, 72)cm (24½ (26¼, 28¼)ins.) from the cast-on edge, ending with a wrong-side row.

SHAPE SHOULDERS

Cast (bind) off 24 (29, 34) stitches at the beginning of the next 2 rows.
Place remaining 23 (33, 43) stitches on a holder.

LEFT FRONT

Rejoin yarn to remaining 45 (55, 65) stitches, work in pattern to end.
Work as for Right front, reversing shapings.

sulka: edge-to-edge lace and cable, chunky jacket

Sleeves

With 6mm (US10) needles, cast on 61 (71, 81) stitches.

Knit 2 rows.

MAIN STITCH PATTERN

Row 1 (right side): K1, [yrn, k3, sl1, k2tog, psso, k3, yrn, k1] to end.

Row 2: Purl to end.

Row 3: P1, [k1, yrn, k2, sl1, k2tog, psso, k2, yrn, k1, p1] to end.

Row 4: K1, [p9, k1] to end.

Row 5: P1, [k2, yrn, k1, sl1, k2tog, psso, k1, yrn, k2, p1] to end.

Row 6: Repeat row 4.

Row 7: P1, [k3, yrn, sl1, k2tog, psso, yrn, k3, p1] to end.

Row 8: Purl to end.

These 8 rows form the pattern.

Repeat the last 8 rows until sleeve measures 40 (40, 42)cm (15¾ (15¾, 16½)ins.) from the cast-on edge, ending with a wrong-side row.

Cast (bind) off.

Neck edge

Join shoulder seams.

With right side facing and 5mm (US8) needles, knit 11 (16, 21) stitches from holder at right front, pick up and knit 9 stitches up right front neck, knit 23 (33, 43) stitches from holder at back, pick up and knit 9 stitches down left front neck, knit 11 (16, 21) stitches from holder at left front. *(63 (83, 103) stitches)*

Knit one row.

Cast (bind) off.

Finishing

Sew on sleeves, placing centre of sleeves to shoulder seams.

Join the sleeve seams.

Weave in ends.

Attach decorative clasp to fasten neck edge as shown in photograph on page 44.

SAMP'A
lace-ribbed, hooded jacket

The lace in this jacket makes it very cooling to wear, while the ribbing and the slight shaping give the garment a flattering fitted look. The partnering of the lace with the hood means this jacket looks just as good with either a floral dress or t-shirt and jeans.

MEASUREMENTS

To fit bust	76.5–81.5	81.5–86.5	91.5–96.5	96.5–101.5	106.5–112	cm
(suggested)	30 32	32–34	36–38	38–40	42–44	ins.
Actual	84	92.5	101	109	117.5	cm
measurement	33	36½	39¾	43	46¼	ins.
Length	67	67	68	70	72	cm
	26½	26½	26¾	27½	28¼	ins.
Sleeve length	26	26	26	26	26	cm
	10¼	10¼	10¼	10¼	10¼	ins.

MATERIALS
13 (14, 15, 16, 17) 50g (1¾oz) balls of
    Samp'a
(photographed in Berry Red, shade 004)

Open ended zip to fit

NEEDLES
One long circular 3.25mm (US3)
    knitting needle
One pair of 3.75mm (US5) knitting needles
Three stitch holders
Knitter's sewing needle or tapestry needle

TENSION (GAUGE)
24 stitches and 30 rows to 10cm (4ins.)
square over pattern using 3.75mm (US5)
needles.

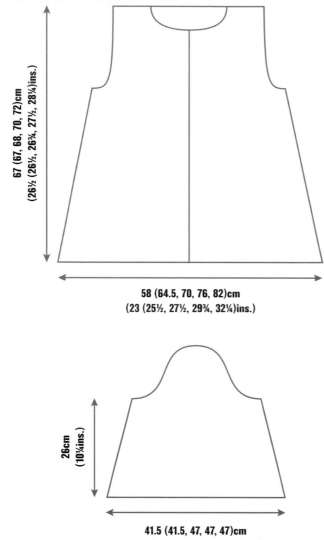

67 (67, 68, 70, 72)cm
(26½ (26½, 26¾, 27½, 28¼)ins.)

58 (64.5, 70, 76, 82)cm
(23 (25½, 27½, 29¾, 32¼)ins.)

26cm
(10¼ins.)

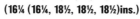

41.5 (41.5, 47, 47, 47)cm
(16¼ (16¼, 18½, 18½, 18½)ins.)

Back

With 3.75mm (US5) needles, cast on 141 (155, 169, 183, 197) stitches.

CABLE LACE PATTERN

Rows 1, 3, and 5 (wrong side): P2, k4, [p3, k4] to last 2 stitches, p2.

Row 2 (right side): K2, p4, [yrn, sl1, k2tog, psso, yrn, p4, k3, p4] to last 9 stitches, yrn, sl1, k2tog, psso, yrn, p4, k2.

Row 4: K2, p4, [k1, yrn, sl1, k1, psso, p4, k3, p4] to last 9 stitches, k1, yrn, sl1, k1, psso, p4, k2.

Row 6: K2, p4, [k3, p4] to last 2 stitches, k2.

These last 6 rows form the cable lace pattern. Repeat the last 6 rows until the back measures 20 (20, 21, 22, 24)cm (7¾ (7¾, 8¼, 8¾, 9½)ins.) from the cast-on edge, ending with row 6 of the cable lace pattern repeat.

Decrease row (wrong side): P2, k2, k2tog, [p3, k2, k2tog] to last 2 stitches, p2.
(121 (133, 145, 157, 169) stitches)

Row 1 (right side): K2, p3, [yrn, sl1, k2tog, psso, yrn, p3, k3, p3] to last 8 stitches, yrn, sl1, k2tog, psso, yrn, p3, k2.

Rows 2, 4, and 6 (wrong side): P2, k3, [p3, k3] to last 2 stitches, p2.

Row 3: K2, P3, [k1, yrn, sl1, k1, psso, p3, k3, p3] to last 8 stitches, k1, yrn, sl1, k1, psso, p3, k2.

Row 5: K2, P3, [k3, p3] to last 2 stitches, k2.

These last 6 rows form the pattern. Repeat the last 6 rows until the back measures 35 (35, 36, 38, 40)cm (13¾ (13¾, 14¼, 15, 15¾)ins.) from the cast-on edge, ending with row 5 of the pattern repeat.

Decrease row (wrong side): P2, k1, k2tog, [p3, k1, k2tog] to last 2 stitches, p2.
(101 (111, 121, 131, 141) stitches)

Row 1 (right side): K2, p2, [yrn, sl1, k2tog, psso, yrn, p2, k3, p2] to last 7 stitches, yrn, sl1, k2tog, psso, yrn, p2, k2.

Rows 2, 4, and 6 (wrong side): P2, k2, [p3, k2] to last 2 stitches, p2.

Row 3: K2, p2, [k1, yrn, sl1, k1, psso, p2, k3, p2] to last 7 stitches, k1, yrn, sl1, k1, psso, p2, k2.

Row 5: K2, p2, [k3, p2] to last 2 stitches, k2. These last 6 rows form the pattern.
Repeat the last 6 rows until the back measures 45 (45, 46, 46, 48)cm (17¾ (17¾,18, 18, 18¾)ins) from the cast-on edge, ending with a wrong-side row.

SHAPE ARMHOLES

Cast (bind) off 5 stitches at the beginning of the next 2 rows.
(91 (101, 111, 121, 131) stitches)
Decrease one stitch at each end of next and 5 following 4th rows.
(79 (89, 99, 109, 119) stitches)
Keeping pattern correct, continue without shaping until armhole measures 22 (22, 22, 24, 24)cm (8¾ (8¾, 8¾, 9½, 9½)ins.) from start of armhole shaping, ending with a wrong-side row.

SHAPE SHOULDERS

Cast (bind) off 19 (22, 26, 30, 34) stitches at the beginning of the next 2 rows.
Place 41 (45, 47, 49, 51) stitches on a holder.

Left front

With 3.75mm (US5) needles, cast on 72 (79, 86, 93, 100) stitches.

CABLE LACE PATTERN

Rows 1, 3, and 5 (wrong side): [P3, k4] to last 2 stitches, p2.

Row 2 (right side): K2, p0 (4, 0, 4, 0), k0 (3, 0, 3, 0), [p4, yrn, sl1, k2tog, psso, yon, p4, k3] to end.

Row 4: K2, p0 (4, 0, 4, 0), k0 (3, 0, 3, 0), [p4, k1, yrn, sl1, k1, psso, p4, k3] to end.

Row 6: K2, [p4, k3] to end.
These last 6 rows form the cable lace pattern.
Repeat the last 6 rows until the left front measures 20 (20, 21, 22, 24)cm (7¾ (7¾, 8¼, 8¾, 9½)ins.) from the cast-on

edge, ending with row 6 of the cable lace pattern repeat.

Decrease row (wrong side): [P3, k2, k2tog] to last 2 stitches, p2.
(62 (68, 74, 80, 86) stitches)

Row 1 (right side): K2, p0 (3, 0, 3, 0), k0 (3, 0, 3, 0), [p3, yrn, sl1, k2tog, psso, yrn, p3, k3] to end.

Rows 2, 4, and 6 (wrong side): [P3, k3] to last 2 stitches, p2.

Row 3: K2, p0 (3, 0, 3, 0), k0 (3, 0, 3, 0), [p3, k1, yrn, sl1, k1, psso, p3, k3] to end.

Row 5: K2, [p3, k3] to end.

These last 6 rows form the pattern.

Repeat the last 6 rows until the left front measures 35 (35, 36, 38, 40)cm (13¾

(13¾, 14¼, 15, 15¾)ins.) from the cast-on edge, ending with row 5 the pattern repeat.

Decrease row (wrong side): [P3, k1, k2tog] to last 2 stitches, p2.
(52 (57, 62, 67, 72) stitches)

Row 1 (right side): K2, p0 (2, 0, 2, 0), k0 (3, 0, 3, 0), [p2, yrn, sl1, k2tog, psso, yrn, p2, k3] to end.

Rows 2, 4, and 6 (wrong side): [P3, k2] to last 2 stitches, p2.

Row 3: K2, p0 (2, 0, 2, 0), k0 (3, 0, 3, 0), [p2, k1, yrn, sl1, k1, psso, p2, k3] to end.

Row 5: K2, [p2, k3] to end.

These last 6 rows form the pattern.

Repeat the last 6 rows until the left front measures 45 (45, 46, 46, 48)cm (17¾ (17¾, 18, 18, 18¾)ins.) from the cast-on edge, ending with a wrong-side row.

SHAPE ARMHOLE

Cast (bind) off 5 stitches at the beginning of the next row. *(47 (52, 57, 62, 67) stitches)*
Work one row in pattern.

Decrease one stitch at armhole edge of next row and 5 following 4th rows.
(41 (46, 51, 56, 61) stitches)

Continue without shaping in pattern until armhole measures 16 (16, 16, 18, 18)cm (6¼ (6¼, 6¼, 7, 7)ins.) from start of armhole shaping, ending with a right-side row.

SHAPE NECK

Next row (wrong side): Work 16 (18, 19, 20, 21) stitches in pattern, slip these stitches onto a holder, work in pattern to end. *(25 (28, 32, 36, 40) stitches)*

Decrease one stitch at the neck edge of next and every following alternate row until 19 (22, 26, 30, 34) stitches remain.

Continue without shaping in pattern until armhole measures 22 (22, 22, 24, 24)cm (8¾ (8¾, 8¾, 9½, 9½)ins.) from start of armhole shaping, ending with a wrong-side row.

Cast (bind) off.

Right front

With 3.75mm (US5) needles, cast on
72 (79, 86, 93, 100) stitches.

CABLE LACE PATTERN

Rows 1, 3, and 5 (wrong side): P2, [k4,
p3] to end.

Row 2 (right side): [K3, p4, yrn, sl1, k2tog,
psso, yrn, p4] to last 2 (9, 2, 9, 2) stitches,
k0 (3, 0, 3, 0), p0 (4, 0, 4, 0), k2.

Row 4: [K3, p4, k1, yrn, sl1, k1, psso, p4]
to last 2 (9, 2, 9, 2) stitches, k0 (3, 0, 3,
0), p0 (4, 0, 4, 0), k2.

Row 6: [K3, p4] to last 2 stitches, k2.
These last 6 rows form the cable lace pattern.
Repeat the last 6 rows until the right front
measures 20 (20, 21, 22, 24)cm (7¾
(7¾, 8¼, 8¾, 9½)ins.) from the cast-on
edge, ending with row 6 of the cable lace
pattern repeat.

Decrease row (wrong side): P2, [k2, k2tog,
p3] to end. *(62 (68, 74, 80, 86) stitches)*

Row 1 (right side): [K3, p3, yrn, sl1, k2tog,
psso, yrn, p3] to last 2 (8, 2, 8, 2) stitches,
k0 (3, 0, 3, 0), p0 (3, 0, 3, 0), k2.

Rows 2, 4, and 6 (wrong side): P2, [k3,
p3] to end.

Row 3: [K3, p3, k1, yrn, sl1, k1, psso, p3]
to last 2 (8, 2, 8, 2) stitches, k0 (3, 0, 3,
0), p0 (3, 0, 3, 0), k2.

Row 5: [K3, p3] to last 2 stitches, k2.
These last 6 rows form the pattern.
Repeat the last 6 rows until the right front
measures 35 (35, 36, 38, 40)cm (13¾
(13¾, 14¼, 15, 15¾)ins. from the
cast-on edge, ending with row 5 of the
pattern repeat.

Decrease row (wrong side): P2, [k1,
k2tog, p3] to end.
(52 (57, 62, 67, 72) stitches)

Row 1 (right side): [K3, p2, yrn, sl1, k2tog,
psso, yrn, p2] to last 2 (7, 2, 7, 2) stitches,
k0 (3, 0, 3, 0), p0 (2, 0, 2, 0), k2.

Rows 2, 4, and 6 (wrong side): P2, [k2,
p3] to end.

Row 3: [K3, p2, k1, yrn, sl1, k1, psso, p2]
to last 2 (7, 2, 7, 2) stitches, k0 (3, 0, 3,
0), p0 (2, 0, 2, 0), k2.

Row 5: [K3, p2] to last 2 stitches, k2.
These last 6 rows form the pattern.
Work as given for Left front, reversing
armhole and neck shapings.

Sleeves

With 3.75mm (US5) needles, cast on
99 (99, 113, 113, 113) stitches.

CABLE AND LACE PATTERN

Rows 1, 3, and 5 (wrong side): P2, k4,
[p3, k4] to last 2 stitches, p2.

Row 2 (right side): K2, p4, [yrn, sl1, k2tog,
psso, yrn, p4, k3, p4] to last 9 stitches, yrn,
sl1, k2tog, psso, yrn, p4, k2.

Row 4: K2, p4, [k1, yrn, sl1, k1, psso, p4,
k3, p4] to last 9 stitches, k1, yrn, sl1, k1,
psso, p4, k2.

Row 6: K2, p4, [k3, p4] to last 2 stitches, k2.
These last 6 rows form the cable lace pattern.
Repeat the last 6 rows until the sleeve
measures 9cm (3½ins.) from the cast-on
edge, ending with row 6 of the cable lace
pattern repeat.

Decrease row (wrong side): P2, k2, k2tog,
[p3, k2, k2tog] to last 2 stitches, p2.
(85 (85, 97, 97, 97) stitches)

Row 1 (right side): K2, p3, [yrn, sl1, k2tog,
psso, yrn, p3, k3, p3] to last 8 stitches, yrn,
sl1, k2tog, psso, yrn, p3, k2.

Rows, 2, 4, and 5 (wrong side): P2, k3,
[p3, k3] to last 2 stitches, p2.

Row 3: K2, p3, [k1, yrn, sl1, k1, psso, p3,
k3, p3] to last 8 stitches, k1, yrn, sl1, k1,
psso, p3, k2.

Row 5: K2, p3, [k3, p3] to last 2 stitches, k2.
These last 6 rows form the pattern.
Repeat the last 6 rows until the sleeve
measures 18cm (7ins.) from the
cast-on edge, ending with row 5 of
the pattern repeat.

Decrease row (wrong side): P2, k1, k2tog, [p3, k1, k2tog] to last 2 stitches, p2. *(71 (71, 81, 81, 81) stitches)*

Row 1 (right side): K2, p2, [yrn, sl1, k2tog, psso, yrn, p2, k3, p2] to last 7 stitches, yrn, sl1, k2tog, psso, yrn, p2, k2.

Rows, 2, 4, and 5 (wrong side): P2, k2, [p3, k2] to last 2 stitches, p2.

Row 3: K2, p2, [k1, yrn, sl1, k1, psso, p2, k3, p2] to last 7 stitches, k1, yrn, sl1, k1, psso, p2, k2.

Row 5: K2, p2, [k3, p2] to last 2 stitches, k2.
These last 6 rows form the pattern.

Repeat the last 6 rows until sleeve measures 26cm (10¼ins.) from the cast-on edge, ending with a wrong-side row.

SHAPE TOP

Cast (bind) off 5 stitches at the beginning of the next 2 rows.
(61 (61, 71, 71, 71) stitches)

Decrease one stitch at each end of next and 6 following 4th rows.
(47 (47, 57, 57, 57) stitches)

Work one row in pattern.

Decrease one stitch at each end of next and 5 following alternate rows.
(35 (35, 45, 45, 45) stitches)

Work one row in pattern.

Decrease one stitch at each end of next and every following row until 15 (15, 21, 21, 21) stitches remaining.

Cast (bind) off 5 stitches at the beginning of the next 2 rows. *(5 (5, 11, 11, 11) stitches)*

Cast (bind) off remaining stitches.

Hood

Join shoulder seams.

With right side facing and 3.75mm (US5) needles, knit 16 (18, 19, 20, 21) stitches from holder at right front, pick up and knit 13 (14, 14, 12, 13) stitches up right front neck, knit 41 (45, 47, 49, 51) stitches from holder at centre back, pick up and knit 12 (13, 14, 12, 12) stitches down left front neck, knit 16 (18, 19, 20, 21) stitches from holder at left front.
(98 (108, 113, 113, 118) stitches)

Row 1: P3, [k2, p3] to end.

Row 2: K3, [p2, k3] to end.

Repeat the last 2 rows until hood measures 35cm (13¾ins.), ending with a wrong-side row.

Cast (bind) off.

Edging

Join cast (bound) off edges of hood.

With right side facing and using a long circular 3.25mm (US3) needle, pick up and knit 116 (116, 119, 122, 125) stitches up right front opening edge, pick up and knit 74 stitches along right side of hood edging, pick up and knit 74 stitches down left side of hood and pick up and knit 116 (116, 119, 122, 125) stitches down left front opening edge. *(380 (380, 386, 392, 398) stitches)*

Knit one row.

Cast (bind) off.

Finishing

Sew on sleeves, placing centre of sleeves to shoulder seams.

Join the side and sleeve seams.

Position and sew zip into place.

Weave in ends.

MISKI
three-quarter length, cable coat

The cable stitch pattern of this coat creates a beautiful texture and fitted look but the shaping means it falls gently over your hips and thighs.

MEASUREMENTS

To fit bust	81.5–86.5	91.5–96.5	96.5–101.5	106.5–112	117–122	cm
(suggested)	32–34	36–38	38–40	42–44	46–48	ins.
Actual	93	101.5	110	118	126.5	cm
measurement	36½	40	43¼	46½	49¾	ins.
Length	70	70	72	72	72	cm
	27½	27½	28¼	28¼	28¼	ins.
Sleeve length	45	45	45	45	45	cm
	17¾	17¾	17¾	17¾	17¾	ins.

MATERIALS
16 (16, 17, 17, 18) 50g (1¾oz) hanks of Miski in yarn A
One 50g (1¾oz) hank of Miski in yarn B
(photographed in: yarn A, Mississippi, shade 117; yarn B, French Navy, shade 106)

8 large buttons

NEEDLES
One pair of 4mm (US6) knitting needles
One pair of 5mm (US8) knitting needles
Cable needle
Three stitch holders
Knitter's sewing needle or tapestry needle

TENSION (GAUGE)
24 stitches and 24 rows to 10cm (4ins.) square over pattern when slightly stretched using 5mm (US8) needles.

55

C4B: Slip next 2 stitches onto cable needle and hold at back, k2 from left-hand needle, k2 from cable needle.

C4F: Slip next 2 stitches onto cable needle and hold at front, k2 from left-hand needle, k2 from cable needle.

Back

With 5mm (US8) needles and yarn B, cast on 154 (168, 182, 196, 210) stitches. Change to yarn A.

CABLE PATTERN

Row 1 (right side): P3, [k8, p6] to last 11 stitches, k8, p3.

Rows 2 and 4: K3, [p8, k6] to last 11 stitches, p8, k3.

Row 3: P3, [C4B, C4F, p6] to last 11 stitches, C4B, C4F, p3.

These 4 rows form the cable pattern. Repeat the last 4 rows until back measures 18cm (7ins.) from the cast on edge, ending with row 3 of the repeat.

Decrease row (wrong side): K1, k2tog, [p8, k2togtbl, k2, k2tog] to last 11 stitches, p8, k2togtbl, k1.

(132 (144, 156, 168, 180) stitches)

Row 1: P2, [k8, p4] to last 10 stitches, k8, p2.

Rows 2 and 4: K2, [p8, k4] to last 10 stitches, p8, k2.

Row 3: P2, [C4B, C4F, p4] to last 10 stitches, C4B, C4F, p2.

These 4 rows form the pattern. Repeat the last 4 rows until back measures 34cm (13¼ins.) from the cast-on edge, ending with row 3 of the repeat.

Decrease row (wrong side): K2, [p8, k2togtbl, k2tog] to last 10 stitches, p8, k2.

(112 (122, 132, 142, 152) stitches)

Row 1: P2, [k8, p2] to end.

Rows 2 and 4: K2, [p8, k2] to end.

Row 3: P2, [C4B, C4F, p2] to end.

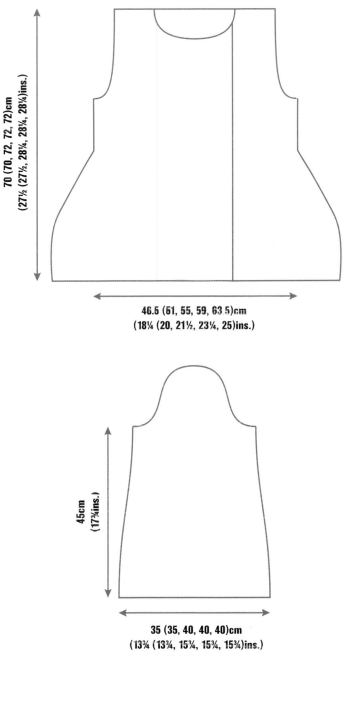

70 (70, 72, 72, 72)cm
(27½ (27½, 28¼, 28¼, 28¼)ins.)

46.5 (51, 55, 59, 63.5)cm
(18¼ (20, 21½, 23¼, 25)ins.)

45cm
(17¾ins.)

35 (35, 40, 40, 40)cm
(13¾ (13¾, 15¾, 15¾, 15¾)ins.)

These 4 rows form the pattern.

Repeat the last 4 rows until back measures 48cm (18¾ins.) from the cast-on edge, ending with a wrong-side row.

SHAPE ARMHOLES

Cast (bind) off 5 stitches at the beginning of the next 2 rows.

(102 (112, 122, 132, 142) stitches)

Decrease one stitch at each end of next and 4 following 4th rows.

(92 (102, 112, 122, 132) stitches)

Continue without shaping in pattern until armhole measures 22 (22, 24, 24, 24)cm (8¾ (8¾, 9½, 9½, 9½)ins.) from start of armhole, ending with a wrong-side row.

SHAPE SHOULDERS

Cast (bind) off 23 (27, 30, 34, 39) stitches at the beginning of the next 2 rows.

Next row: K5 (3, 0, 6, 1), k2 (0, 0, 0, 0)tog, p2, [k2togtbl, k4, k2tog, p2] to last 7 (3, 0, 6, 1) stitches, k2 (0, 0, 0, 0)togtbl, k5 (3, 0, 6, 1).

Place 38 (40, 42, 46, 44) stitches on a stitch holder.

Left front

With 5mm (US8) needles and yarn B, cast on 89 (95, 103, 109, 117) stitches.

Change to yarn A.

CABLE PATTERN

Row 1 (right side): P3, *k8, p6, repeat from * to last 30 (36, 30, 36, 30) stitches, [k4, p2] 5 (6, 5, 6, 5) times.

Rows 2 and 4: [K2, p4] 5 (6, 5, 6, 5) times, *k6, p8, repeat from * to last 3 stitches, k3.

Row 3: P3, *C4B, C4F, p6, repeat from * to last 30 (36, 30, 36, 30) stitches, [k4, p2] 5 (6, 5, 6, 5) times.

These 4 rows form the cable pattern.

Repeat the last 4 rows until left front measures 18cm (7ins.) from the cast-on edge, ending with row 3 of the repeat.

Decrease row (wrong side): [K2, p4] 5 (6, 5, 6, 5) times, *k2togtbl, k2, k2tog, p8, repeat from * to last 3 stitches, k2togtbl, k1.

(80 (86, 92, 98, 104) stitches)

Row 1: P2, *k8, p4, repeat from * to last 30 (36, 30, 36, 30) stitches, [k4, p2] 5 (6, 5, 6, 5) times.

Rows 2 and 4: [K2, p4] 5 (6, 5, 6, 5) times, *k4, p8, repeat from * to last 2 stitches, k2.

Row 3: P2, *C4B, C4F, p4, repeat from * to last 30 (36, 30, 36, 30) stitches, [k4, p2] 5 (6, 5, 6, 5) times.

These 4 rows form the pattern. Repeat the last 4 rows until left front measures 34cm (13¼ins.) from the cast-on edge, ending with row 3 of the repeat.

Decrease row (wrong side): [K2, p4] 5 (6, 5, 6, 5) times, *k2togtbl, k2tog, p8, repeat from * to last 2 stitches, k2.

(72 (78, 82, 88, 92) stitches)

Row 1: P2, *k8, p2, repeat from * to last 30 (36, 30, 36, 30) stitches, [k4, p2] 5 (6, 5, 6, 5) times.

Rows 2 and 4: [K2, p4] 5 (6, 5, 6, 5) times, *k2, p8, repeat from * to last 2 stitches, k2.

Row 3: P2, *C4B, C4F, p2, repeat from * to last 30 (36, 30, 36, 30) stitches, [k4, p2] 5 (6, 5, 6, 5) times.

These 4 rows form the pattern.

Repeat the last 4 rows until left front measures 48cm (18¾ins.) from the cast-on edge, ending with a wrong-side row.

SHAPE ARMHOLE

Cast (bind) off 5 stitches at the beginning of the next row. *(67 (73, 77, 83, 87) stitches)*

Work one row in pattern.

Decrease one stitch at armhole edge of next and 4 following 4th rows.

(62 (68, 72, 78, 82) stitches)

Continue without shaping in pattern until armhole measures 14 (14, 16, 16, 16)cm (5½ (5½, 6¼, 6¼, 6¼)ins.) from start of armhole shaping, ending with a right-side row.

SHAPE NECK

Next row: Work 32 (36, 36, 36, 36)
stitches in pattern, place these stitches on a
holder, work in pattern to end.
(30 (32, 36, 42, 46) stitches)

Decrease one stitch at neck edge of next and
every following alternative row until there are
23 (27, 30, 34, 39) stitches.

Continue without shaping in pattern until
armhole measures 22 (22, 24, 24, 24)cm
(8¾ (8¾, 9½, 9½, 9½)ins.) from start of
armhole shaping ending with a
wrong-side row.

Cast (bind) off.

Mark positions for 3 buttons along front
opening edge, first one 43cm (17ins.) from
the cast-on edge, second one 1cm (½in.)
from cast (bound) off edge, and remaining
button placed evenly between the two.

Right front

With 5mm (US8) needles and yarn B, cast
on 89 (95, 103, 109, 117) stitches.
Change to yarn A.

CABLE PATTERN

Row 1 (right side): [P2, k4] 5 (6, 5, 6, 5)
times, *p6, k8, repeat from * to last
3 stitches, p3.

Rows 2 and 4: K3, *p8, k6, repeat from *
to last 30 (36, 30, 36, 30) stitches, [p4,
k2] 5 (6, 5, 6, 5) times.

Row 3: [P2, k4] 5 (6, 5, 6, 5) times, *p6,
C4B, C4F, repeat from * to last 3 stitches, p3.

These 4 rows form the cable pattern.
Repeat the last 4 rows until right front
measures 18cm (7ins.) from the cast-on
edge, ending with row 3 of the repeat.

Decrease row (wrong side): K1, k2tog,
*p8, k2togtbl, k2, k2tog, repeat from * to
last 30 (36, 30, 36, 30) stitches, [p4, k2]
5 (6, 5, 6, 5) times.
(80 (86, 92, 98, 104) stitches)

Row 1: [P2, k4] 5 (6, 5, 6, 5) times, *p4,
k8, repeat from * to last 2 stitches, p2.

Rows 2 and 4: K2, *p8, k4, repeat from *
to last 30 (36, 30, 36, 30) stitches, [p4,
k2] 5 (6, 5, 6, 5) times.

Row 3: [P2, k4] 5 (6, 5, 6, 5) times, *p4,
C4B, C4F, repeat from * to last 2 stitches, p2.

These 4 rows form the pattern. Repeat the
last 4 rows until right front measures 34cm
(13¼ins.) from the cast-on edge, ending
with row 3 of the repeat.

Decrease row (wrong side): K2, *p8,
k2togtbl, k2tog, repeat from * to last
30 (36, 30, 36, 30) stitches, [p4, k2]
5 (6, 5, 6, 5) times.
(72 (78, 82, 88, 92) stitches)

Row 1: [P2, k4] 5 (6, 5, 6, 5) times, *p2,
k8, repeat from * to last 2 stitches, p2.

Rows 2 and 4: K2, *p8, k2, repeat from *
to last 30 (36, 30, 36, 30) stitches, [p4,
k2] 5 (6, 5, 6, 5) times.

Row 3: [P2, k4] 5 (6, 5, 6, 5) times, *p2,
C4B, C4F, repeat from * to last 2 stitches, p2.

These 4 rows form the pattern.

Work as given for the Left front, reversing
shaping and working buttonholes as below
to correspond with positions marked on
left front.

Buttonhole row 1 (right side): P2, k1, cast
(bind) off 2 stitches (1 stitch on right needle
after cast off), p2, [k4, p2] twice, k1, cast
(bind) off 2 stitches, work in pattern to end.

Buttonhole row 2 (wrong side): Work in
pattern to end, casting on 2 stitches over
those cast (bound) off on previous row.

Sleeves

With 5mm (US8) needles and yarn B, cast on 84 (84, 96, 96, 96) stitches.

Change to yarn A.

CABLE PATTERN

Row 1 (right side): P2, [k8, p4] to last 10 stitches, k8, p2.

Rows 2 and 4: K2, [p8, k4] to last 10 stitches, p8, k2.

Row 3: P2, [C4B, C4F, p4] to last 10 stitches, C4B, C4F, p2.

These 4 rows form the cable pattern. Repeat the last 4 rows until sleeve measures 10cm (4ins.) from the cast-on edge, ending with row 3 of the repeat.

Decrease row (wrong side): K2, [p8, k2togtbl, k2tog] to last 10 stitches, p8, k2.

(72 (72, 82, 82, 82) stitches)

Row 1: P2, [k8, p2] to end.

Rows 2 and 4: K2, [p8, k2] to end.

Row 3: P2, [C4B, C4F, p2] to end.

These 4 rows form the pattern.

Repeat the last 4 rows until sleeve measures 45cm (17¾ins.) from the cast-on edge, ending with a wrong-side row.

SHAPE TOP

Cast (bind) off 5 stitches at the beginning of the next 2 rows.

(62 (62, 72, 72, 72) stitches)

Decrease one stitch at each end of next and 5 following 4th rows.

(50 (50, 60, 60, 60) stitches)

Work 3 rows in pattern.

Decrease one stitch at each end of next and 4 following alternate rows.

(40 (40, 50, 50, 50) stitches)

Work one row in pattern.

Decrease one stitch at each end of next and every following row until 18 (18, 20, 20, 20) stitches remain.

Cast (bind) off 5 stitches at the beginning of the next 2 rows. *(8 (8, 10, 10, 10) stitches)*

Cast (bind) off remaining stitches.

Collar

Join shoulder seams.

With right side facing, 4mm (US6) needles and yarn A, rib 32 (36, 36, 36, 36) stitches from holder at right front, pick up and knit 16 (13, 16, 18, 15) stitches up right front neck, rib 38 (40, 42, 46, 44) stitches from holder at the back, pick up and knit 16 (13, 16, 18, 15) stitches down left front neck, rib 32 (36, 36, 36, 36) stitches from holder at left front.

(134 (138, 146, 154, 146) stitches)

RIB PATTERN

Row 1 (wrong side): [K2, p4] 5 (6, 6, 6, 6) times, *k2, p6, repeat from * to last 32 (38, 38, 38, 38) stitches, k2, [p4, k2] to end.

Row 2: [P2, k4] 5 (6, 6, 6, 6) times, *p2, k6, repeat from * to last 32 (38, 38, 38, 38) stitches, p2, [k4, p2] to end.

These 2 rows form the rib pattern.

Repeat the last 2 rows until collar measures 8cm (3¼ins.), ending with a wrong-side row.

Work the buttonhole rows 1 and 2 as given for the right front.

Work in rib pattern until collar measures 12cm (4¾ins.), ending with a right-side row.

Change to yarn B.

Work one row in rib.

Cast (bind) off with yarn B.

Finishing

Sew on sleeves, placing centre of sleeves to shoulder seams.

Join the side and sleeve seams.

Position and sew buttons into place.

Weave in ends.

miska: three-quarter length, cable coat

2 Sweaters

textured stripe, loose-fitting sweater
page 64

zig zag, high-collared sweater
page 68

sweater with elongated neck-opening
page 72

sloppy-joe inspired, raglan sweater
page 77

ruffly-stripes, wide-neck sweater
page 81

K'ACHA

textured stripe, loose-fitting sweater

This sweater plays with a basic rib. One row is replaced with a knit row and another with lace, to create this loose-fitting garment.

MEASUREMENTS

To fit bust	81.5–86.5	91.5–96.5	96.5–101.5	106.5–112	117–122	cm
(suggested)	32–34	36–38	38–40	42–44	46–48	ins.
Actual	102	106	114	122	130	cm
measurement	40	41¾	45	48	51	ins.
Length	62	62	76	76	76	cm
	24½	24½	30	30	30	ins.
Sleeve length	46	46	46	46	46	cm
	18	18	18	18	18	ins.

MATERIALS

12 (13, 13, 14, 14) 50g (1¾oz) hanks of
    K'acha in yarn A
One 50g (1¾oz) hank of K'acha in yarn B
(photographed in: yarn A, Trinity Cream,
shade 1200; yarn B, Dark Chocolate,
shade 1205)

NEEDLES

One pair of 4mm (US6) knitting needles
Knitter's sewing needle or tapestry needle

TENSION (GAUGE)

20 stitches and 30 rows to 10cm (4ins.)
square over garter stitch rib pattern using
4mm (US6) needles.

Back and front alike

With 4mm (US6) needles and yarn B, cast
on 102 (106, 114, 122, 130) stitches.
Change to yarn A.

LACE PATTERN

Row 1 (right side): K1, *k2tog, [yrn] twice,
sl1, k1, psso, repeat from * to last stitch, k1.
Row 2: P1, *p1, [k1, p1] into double yrn,
p1, repeat from * to last stitch, p1.
These 2 rows form the lace rib pattern.
Repeat the last 2 rows a further 8 times.

GARTER STITCH RIB PATTERN

Row 1: Knit to end.
Row 2: P2, [k2, p2] to end.
These 2 rows form the garter stitch
rib pattern.
Repeat the last 2 rows a further 8 times.
The last 36 rows form the pattern repeat.
Repeat the last 36 rows 3 (3, 4, 4, 4)
times more.

SHAPE ONE NECK AND SHOULDER

Next row: Work 28 (30, 33, 37, 40)
stitches in pattern, turn and place remaining
74 (76, 81, 85, 90) stitches on a holder.

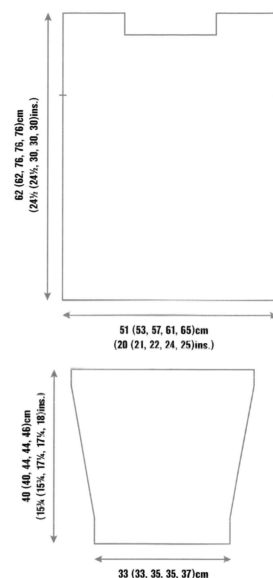

62 (62, 76, 76, 76)cm
(24½ (24½, 30, 30, 30)ins.)

51 (53, 57, 61, 65)cm
(20 (21, 22, 24, 25)ins.)

40 (40, 44, 44, 46)cm
(15¾ (15¾, 17¼, 17¼, 18)ins.)

33 (33, 35, 35, 37)cm
(13 (13, 13¾, 13¾, 14½)ins.)

Work in garter stitch rib pattern on these 28 (30, 33, 37, 40) stitches until it measures 5cm (2ins.).
Cast (bind) off.

SHAPE THE OTHER NECK AND SHOULDER

With right side facing, cast (bind) off centre 46 (46, 48, 48, 50) stitches purlwise, work in pattern to end.
Work to match one neck and shoulder.

Sleeves

With 4mm (US6) needles and yarn B, cast on 66 (66, 70, 70, 74) stitches.
Change to yarn A.
Starting with a row 1 of the Back and front alike lace pattern, continue in pattern until sleeve measures 5cm (2ins.) from the cast-on edge, ending with a wrong-side row.
Keeping pattern correct, increase one stitch at each end of next and every following 6th row until there are 86 (86, 90, 90, 94) stitches.
Continue without shaping in pattern until sleeve measures 46cm (18ins.) from the cast-on edge, ending with a wrong-side row.
Cast (bind) off.

Finishing

Join shoulder seams.
Sew on sleeves, placing centre of sleeves to shoulder seams.
Join the side and sleeve seams.
Weave in ends.

k'acha: textured stripe, loose-fitting sweater

SULKA
zig zag, high-collared sweater

The zig zag or chevron is a favourite motif of mine. Using a very tactile yarn, this sweater uses stitches to create a subtle zig zag.

MEASUREMENTS

To fit bust	81.5–86.5	91.5–96.5	96.5–101.5	106.5–112	117–122	cm
(suggested)	32–34	36–38	38–40	42–44	46–48	ins.
Actual	91	101	111	121	131	cm
measurement	35¾	39¾	43¾	47½	51½	ins.
Length	67	67	72	72	74	cm
	26½	26½	28¼	28¼	29	ins.
Sleeve length	45	45	45	45	45	cm
	17¾	17¾	17¾	17¾	17¾	ins.

MATERIALS
23 (23, 24, 24, 25) 50g (1¾oz) hanks of
    Sulka in yarn A
One 50g (1¾oz) hank of Sulka in yarn B
(photographed in: yarn A, Red Onion, shade
222; yarn B, Lime, shade 202)

NEEDLES
One pair of 5mm (US8) knitting needles
One pair of 6mm (US10) knitting needles
Two stitch holders
Knitter's sewing needle or tapestry needle

TENSION (GAUGE)
16 stitches and 24 rows to 10cm (4ins.)
square over chevron pattern using 6mm
(US10) needles.

Back and front alike
With 6mm (US10) needles and yarn B, cast
on 73 (81, 89, 97, 105) stitches.
Change to yarn A.

CHEVRON PATTERN
Row 1 (right side): K1, [p7, k1] to end.
Row 2: P1, [k7, p1] to end.
Row 3: K2, [p5, k3] to last 7 stitches,
p5, k2.
Row 4: P2, [k5, p3] to last 7 stitches,
k5, p2.
Row 5: K3, [p3, k5] to last 6 stitches,
p3, k3.
Row 6: P3, [k3, p5] to last 6 stitches,
k3, p3.
Row 7: K4, [p1, k7] to last 5 stitches,
p1, k4.
Row 8: P4, [k1, p7] to last 5 stitches,
k1, p4.
Row 9: Repeat row 2.
Row 10: Repeat row 1.
Row 11: Repeat row 4.

Row 12: Repeat row 3.

Row 13: Repeat row 6.

Row 14: Repeat row 5.

Row 15: Repeat row 8.

Row 16: Repeat row 7.

These 16 rows form the chevron pattern. Repeat the last 16 rows until work measures 45 (45, 48, 48, 50)cm (17¾ (17¾, 18¾, 18¾, 19½)ins.) from the cast-on edge, ending with a wrong-side row.

SHAPE ARMHOLES

Cast (bind) off 4 stitches at the beginning of the next 2 rows.

(65 (73, 81, 89, 97) stitches)

Decrease one stitch at each end of next and 3 following 4th rows.

(57 (65, 73, 81, 89) stitches)

Continue without shaping in chevron pattern until armhole measures 14 (14, 16, 16, 16)cm (5½ (5½, 6¼, 6¼, 6¼)ins.) from start of armhole shaping, ending with a wrong-side row.

SHAPE LEFT NECK

Next row: Work in pattern until there are 20 (24, 27, 30, 34) stitches on right-hand needle, place remaining stitches on a stitch holder, turn.

Work one row in pattern.

Decrease one stitch at neck edge of next and every following alternate rows until there are 14 (18, 21, 24, 28) stitches.

Continue without shaping in chevron pattern until armhole measures 22 (22, 24, 24, 24)cm (8¾ (8¾, 9½, 9½, 9½)ins.) from start of armhole shaping, ending with a wrong-side row.

Cast (bind) off.

SHAPE RIGHT NECK

With right side facing, leave centre 17 (17, 19, 21, 21) stitches on a stitch holder, rejoin yarn to remaining 20 (24, 27, 30, 34) stitches, work in pattern to end.

Work to match left neck, reversing shapings.

Sleeves

With 6mm (US10) needles and yarn B, cast on 57 (57, 65, 65, 65) stitches.

Change to yarn A.

Starting with row 1 of chevron pattern as given for the Back and front alike, continue in chevron pattern until sleeve measures 45cm (17¾ins.) from the cast-on edge, ending with a wrong-side row.

SHAPE TOP

Cast (bind) off 4 stitches at the beginning of the next 2 rows.

(49 (49, 57, 57, 57) stitches)

Decrease one stitch at each end of next and 5 following 4th rows.

(37 (37, 45, 45, 45) stitches)

Work one row in pattern.

Decrease one stitch at each end of next and 4 following alternate rows.

(27 (27, 35, 35, 35) stitches)

Work one row in pattern.

Decrease one stitch at each end of next and every following row until there are 9 (9, 11, 11, 11) stitches.

Cast (bind) off 3 (3, 4, 4, 4) stitches at the beginning of the next 2 rows. *(3 stitches)*

Cast (bind) off remaining stitches.

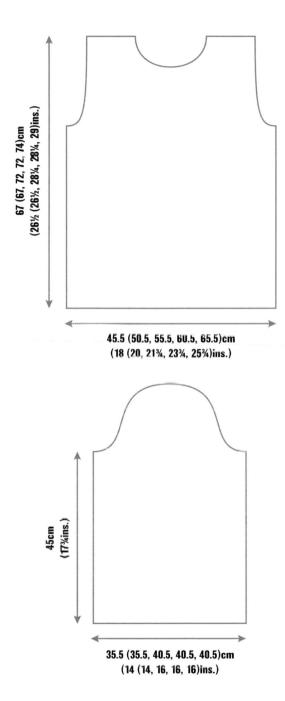

67 (67, 72, 72, 74)cm
(26½ (26½, 28¼, 28¼, 29)ins.)

45.5 (50.5, 55.5, 60.5, 65.5)cm
(18 (20, 21¾, 23¾, 25¾)ins.)

45cm
(17¾ins.)

35.5 (35.5, 40.5, 40.5, 40.5)cm
(14 (14, 16, 16, 16)ins.)

Collar

Join right shoulder seam.

With right side facing, 5mm (US8) needles and yarn A, pick up and knit 12 (12, 13, 12, 12) stitches down left front neck, knit 17 (17, 19, 21, 21) stitches from holder at centre front, pick up and knit 12 (12, 13, 12, 12) stitches up right front neck, pick up and knit 11 (11, 12, 11, 11) stitches down right back neck, knit 17 (17, 19, 21, 21) stitches from holder at back, pick up and knit 12 (12, 13, 12, 12) stitches up left back neck. *(81 (81, 89, 89, 89) stitches)*

Change to 6mm (US10) needles.

Starting with row 1, continue in chevron pattern as given for the Back and front alike, until collar measures 30cm (11¾ins.), ending with a wrong-side row.

Cast (bind) off knitwise in yarn B.

Finishing

Join left shoulder seam and collar edge, reversing seam half way.

Sew on sleeves, placing centre of sleeves to shoulder seams.

Join the side and sleeve seams.

Weave in ends.

MISKI

sweater with elongated neck-opening

The simple notion of using a different contrasting edging on a garment with a deep neck-opening, creates a sweater with zing!

MEASUREMENTS

To fit bust	81.5–86.5	91.5–96.5	96.5–101.5	106.5–112	117–122	cm
(suggested)	32–34	36–38	38–40	42–44	46–48	ins.
Actual	94	100	105.5	111	116.5	cm
measurement	37	39¼	41½	43¾	45¾	ins.
Length	77	77	79	82	82	cm
	30¼	30¼	31	32¼	32¼	ins.
Sleeve length	45	45	45	45	45	cm
	17¾	17¾	17¾	17¾	17¾	ins.

MATERIALS

16 (17, 17, 18, 18) 50g (1¾oz) hanks of
    Miski in yarn A
1 (1, 1, 2, 2) 50g (1¾oz) hank(s) of
    Miski in yarn B
(photographed in: yarn A, Black Beauty,
shade 115; yarn B, Orchid, shade 119)

8 small buttons

NEEDLES

One pair of 4.5mm (US7) knitting needles
One pair of 5mm (US8) knitting needles
Knitter's sewing needle or tapestry needle

TENSION (GAUGE)

18 stitches and 28 rows to 10cm (4ins.)
square over garter stitch pattern using 5mm
(US8) needles.

Back

With 5mm (US8) needles and yarn B, cast
on 85 (90, 95, 100, 105) stitches.
Change to yarn A.

EDGE PATTERN

Row 1 (right side): Knit to end.
Row 2: K2, p1, [k4, p1] to last 2 stitches, k2.
These 2 rows form the edge pattern.
Repeat the last 2 rows until back measures
20 (20, 20, 25, 25)cm (7¾ (7¾, 7¾,
9¾, 9¾)ins.) from the cast-on edge, ending
with a wrong-side row.

MAIN PATTERN

Row 1 (right side): K2, p1, [k4, p1] to last
2 stitches, k2.
Row 2: Knit to end.
These 2 rows form the main pattern.
Repeat the last 2 rows until back measures
55 (55, 55, 58, 58)cm (21½ (21½, 21½,
22¾, 22¾)ins.) from the cast-on edge,
ending with a wrong-side row.

SHAPE ARMHOLES

Cast (bind) off 4 stitches at the beginning of the next 2 rows.
(77 (82, 87, 92, 97) stitches)
Decrease one stitch at each end of next and 3 following 4th rows.
(69 (74, 79, 84, 89) stitches)
Continue without shaping in main pattern until armhole measures 22 (22, 24, 24, 24)cm (8¾ (8¾, 9½, 9½, 9½)ins.) from start of armhole shaping, ending with a wrong-side row.

SHAPE SHOULDERS

Cast (bind) off 17 (19, 21, 22, 24) stitches at the beginning of the next 2 rows.
Place the remaining 35 (36, 37, 40, 41) stitches on a stitch holder.

Front

With 5mm (US8) needles and yarn B, cast on 85 (90, 95, 100, 105) stitches.
Change to yarn A.

EDGE PATTERN

Row 1 (right side): Knit to end.
Row 2: K2, p1, [k4, p1] to last 2 stitches, k2.
These 2 rows form the edge pattern.
Repeat the last 2 rows until front measures 20 (20, 20, 25, 25)cm (7¾ (7¾, 7¾, 9¾, 9¾)ins.) from the cast-on edge, ending with a wrong-side row.
Starting with row 1 of main pattern given for Back, continue in main pattern shaping left side as follows:

SHAPE LEFT SIDE

Next row: Work in main pattern until there are 42 (45, 47, 50, 52) stitches on the right hand needle, slip remaining stitches onto a stitch holder, turn and work in main pattern to end.

Continue in main pattern on these 42 (45, 47, 50, 52) stitches until front measures 55 (55, 55, 58, 58)cm (21½ (21½, 21½, 22¾, 22¾)ins.) from the cast-on edge, ending with a wrong-side row.

SHAPE ARMHOLE

Cast (bind) off 4 stitches at the beginning of the next row. *(38 (41, 43, 46, 48) stitches)*
Work one row in pattern.

Decrease one stitch at the armhole edge of next row and 3 following 4th rows.
(34 (37, 39, 42, 44) stitches)

Continue without shaping in main pattern until armhole measures 16 (16, 18, 18, 18)cm (6¼ (6¼, 7, 7, 7)ins.) from start of armhole shaping, ending with a right-side row.

SHAPE LEFT NECK

Next row: Work 11 stitches in pattern, slip these stitches onto a stitch holder, work in pattern to end.
(23 (26, 28, 31, 33) stitches)

Work one row in pattern.

Decrease one stitch at neck edge of the next and every following row until 17 (19, 21, 22, 24) stitches remain.

Continue without shaping in main pattern, until armhole measures 22 (22, 24, 24, 24)cm (8¾ (8¾, 9½, 9½, 9½)ins.) from start of armhole shaping, ending with a wrong-side row.
Cast (bind) off.

SHAPE RIGHT SIDE

With right side facing, cast (bind) off 1 (0, 1, 0, 1) stitch, rejoin yarn to remaining 42 (45, 47, 50, 52) stitches, work in pattern to end.

Work as given for left side, reversing shapings.

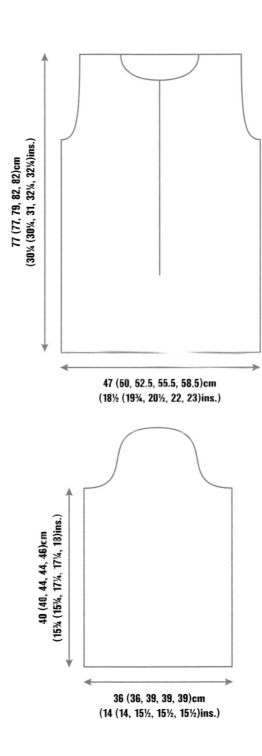

77 (77, 79, 82, 82)cm
(30¼ (30¼, 31, 32¼, 32¼)ins.)

47 (50, 52.5, 55.5, 58.5)cm
(18½ (19¾, 20½, 22, 23)ins.)

40 (40, 44, 44, 46)cm
(15¾ (15¾, 17¼, 17¼, 18)ins.)

36 (36, 39, 39, 39)cm
(14 (14, 15½, 15½, 15½)ins.)

Sleeves

With 5mm (US8) needles and yarn B, cast on 65 (65, 70, 70, 70) stitches.

Change to yarn A.

Starting with a row 1 of main pattern as given for the Back, continue in main pattern until sleeve measures 45cm (17¾ins.) from the cast-on edge, ending with a wrong-side row.

SHAPE TOP

Cast (bind) off 4 stitches at the beginning of the next 2 rows.

(57, 57, 62, 62, 62) stitches)

Decrease one stitch at each end of next and 5 following 4th rows.

(45 (45, 50, 50, 50) stitches)

Work 3 rows in pattern.

Decrease one stitch at each end of next and 4 following alternate rows.

(35 (35, 40, 40, 40) stitches)

Work one row in pattern.

Decrease one stitch at each end of next and every following row until 19 (19, 20, 20, 20) stitches remain.

Cast (bind) off 5 stitches at the beginning of the next 2 rows. *(9 (9, 10, 10, 10) stitches)*

Cast (bind) off remaining stitches.

Left edging

Join shoulder seams.

With right side facing, 4.5mm (US7) needles and yarn B, pick up and knit 105 stitches down left front opening edge.

Knit one row.

Cast (bind) off.

Right edging

With right side facing, 4.5mm (US7) needles and yarn B, pick up and knit 105 stitches up right front opening edge.

Buttonhole row (wrong side): K9, [k2tog, yon, k10] to end.

Cast (bind) off loosely over yon.

Neck

With right side facing, 4.5mm (US7) needles and yarn B, pick up and knit 2 stitches from edging, knit 11 stitches from holder at right front, pick up and knit 17 stitches up right front neck, knit 35 (36, 37, 40, 41) stitches from holder at the back, pick up and knit 17 stitches down left front neck, knit 11 stitches from holder at left front, pick up and knit 2 stitches from edging.

(95 (96, 97, 100, 101) stitches)

Knit one row.

Cast (bind) off.

Finishing

Sew on sleeves, placing centre of sleeves to shoulder seams.

Join the side and sleeve seams.

Slip stitch edging ends into place with right edging over left edging.

Position and sew buttons into place.

Weave in ends.

AKAPANA
sloppy-joe inspired, raglan sweater

This sweater is a hybrid – a sloppy-joe with shaping. It has the relaxed comfort of a sloppy-joe but texture and raglan shaping give it that unique hand-knitted feel.

MEASUREMENTS

To fit bust	86.5–91.5	96.5–101.5	106.5–112	117–122	127–132	cm
(suggested)	34–36	38–40	42–44	46–48	50–52	ins.
Actual	106.5	117.5	128.5	140	151	cm
measurement	42	46¼	50½	55	59½	ins.
Length	75	76	76.5	79	79.5	cm
	29½	30	30	31	31¼	ins.
Sleeve length	45	45	45	45	45	cm
	17¾	17¾	17¾	17¾	17¾	ins.

MATERIALS
16 (17, 18, 19, 20) 50g (1¾oz) hanks of
   Akapana
(photographed in Moche Turquoise,
shade 1304)

NEEDLES
One pair of 4mm (US6) knitting needles
One pair of 4.5mm (US7) knitting needles
Three stitch holders
Knitter's sewing needle or tapestry needle

TENSION (GAUGE)
18 stitches and 26 rows to 10cm (4ins.)
square over stocking (stockinette) stitch
using 4.5mm (US7) needles.

77

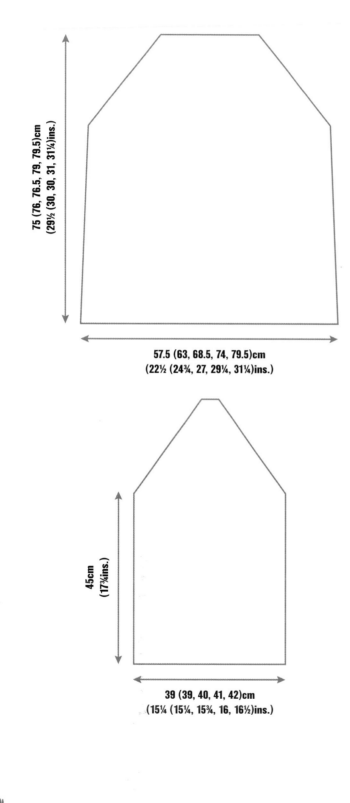

75 (76, 76.5, 79, 79.5)cm
(29½ (30, 30, 31, 31¼)ins.)

57.5 (63, 68.5, 74, 79.5)cm
(22½ (24¾, 27, 29¼, 31¼)ins.)

45cm
(17¾ins.)

39 (39, 40, 41, 42)cm
(15¼ (15¼, 15¾, 16, 16½)ins.)

Back and front alike

With 4.5mm (US7) needles, cast on
116 (126, 136, 146, 156) stitches.
Rows 1 and 3 (right side): P29 (34, 39,
44, 49), k4, [p14, k4] 3 times, purl to end.
Row 2: K29 (34, 39, 44, 49), p4, *k1,
[k1, p1, k1 all into the same stitch, p3tog]
3 times, k1, p4, repeat from * until there are
29 (34, 39, 44, 49) stitches, knit to end.
Row 4: K29 (34, 39, 44, 49), p4,
*k1, [p3tog, k1, p1, k1 all into the same
stitch] 3 times, k1, p4, repeat from * until
there are 29 (34, 39, 44, 49) stitches,
knit to end.
Repeat the last 4 rows until back measures
20cm (7¾ins.) from the cast-on edge,
ending with a 4th row.
Next row (right side): P29 (34, 39, 44,
49), k2tog, k2, [p14, k2tog, k2] 3 times,
purl to end.
(112 (122, 132, 142, 152) stitches)
Row 1: K29 (34, 39, 44, 49), p3, *k1,
[k1, p1, k1 all into the same stitch, p3tog]
3 times, k1, p3, repeat from * until there are
29 (34, 39, 44, 49) stitches, knit to end.
Rows 2 and 4 (right side): P29 (34, 39,
44, 49), k3, [p14, k3] 3 times, purl to end.
Row 3: K29 (34, 39, 44, 49), p3,
*k1, [p3tog, k1, p1, k1 all into the same
stitch] 3 times, k1, p3, repeat from * until
there are 29 (34, 39, 44, 49) stitches,
knit to end.
Repeat the last 4 rows until back measures
38cm (15ins.) from the cast-on edge,
ending with a 3rd row.
Next row (right side): P29 (34, 39, 44,
49), k2tog, k1, [p14, k2tog, k1] 3 times,
purl to end.
(108 (118, 128, 138, 148) stitches)
Row 1: K29 (34, 39, 44, 49), p2,
*k1, [k1, p1, k1 all into the same stitch,
p3tog] 3 times, k1, p2, repeat from * until
there are 29 (34, 39, 44, 49) stitches, knit
to end.

akapana: sloppy-joe inspired, raglan, sweater

Rows 2 and 4 (right side): P29 (34, 39, 44, 49), k2, [p14, k2] 3 times, purl to end.

Row 3: K29 (34, 39, 44, 49), p2, *k1, [p3tog, k1, p1, k1 all into the same stitch] 3 times, k1, p2, repeat from * until there are 29 (34, 39, 44, 49) stitches, knit to end.

Repeat the last 4 rows until back measures 52cm (20½ins.) from the cast-on edge, ending with a wrong-side row.

SHAPE RAGLANS

Decrease row (right side): K1, k2togtbl, work in the pattern to last 3 stitches, k2tog, k1.

(106 (116, 126, 136, 146) stitches)

Next row: P2 (2, 1, 1, 1), [p2tog] 0 (0, 1, 1, 1) times work in the pattern to last 2 (2, 3, 3, 3) stitches, [p2togtbl] 0 (0, 1,1,1) times, p2 (2,1,1,1).

(106 (116, 124, 134, 144) stitches)

These 2 rows set the position of the decrease, with stocking (stockinette) stitch panel.

SIZE EXTRA SMALL ONLY

Decrease one stitch as set above on each end of 3rd and following 4th row.

SIZE SMALL ONLY

Decrease one stitch as set above on each end of 3rd row only.

SIZES MEDIUM, LARGE, AND EXTRA LARGE ONLY

Decrease one stitch as set above on each end of the next row only.

ALL SIZES

Work one row in the pattern.

(102 (114, 122, 132, 142) stitches)

Decrease one stitch as set above on each end of next and every following alternate row until there are 52 (58, 62, 66, 74) stitches, ending with a wrong-side row.

Place the remaining stitches on a holder.

Sleeves

With 4.5mm (US7) needles, cast on 70 (70, 72, 74, 76) stitches.

Starting with a purl row, continue in reverse stocking (stockinette) stitch until sleeve measure 45cm (17¾ins.) from the cast-on edge, ending with a wrong-side row.

SHAPE RAGLANS

Decrease one stitch as set for back on next and every following alternate row until there are 10 (8, 8, 4, 4) stitches.

Leave these stitches on a holder.

Neck edging

Join raglan seams leaving left front open.

With right side facing and 4mm (US6) needles, pick up and knit 52 (58, 62, 66, 74) stitches from centre front neck, knit 10 (8, 8, 4, 4) stitches from holder at sleeve and pick up and knit 52 (58, 62, 66, 74) stitches from holder from the back, knit 10 (8, 8, 4, 4) stitches from holder at sleeve.

(124 (132, 140, 140, 156) stitches)

Next row: [K4, k2tog] to last 4 (0, 2, 2, 0) stitches, k4 (0, 2, 2, 0).

(104 (110, 117, 117, 130) stitches)

Knit 4 rows.

Cast (bind) off.

Finishing

Join the left raglan and neck edging seam.

Join the side and sleeve seams.

Weave in ends.

NUNA

ruffly-stripes, wide-neck sweater

This is a striped sweater with a difference. Each stripe-band uses one of two needle sizes and increases and decreases to create ruffly-stripes. There are a few moments where concentration is needed in this pattern, but I feel that the end result makes it worth it.

MEASUREMENTS

To fit bust	81.5–86	86–91.5	96.5–101.5	101.5–106.5	111.5–116.5	cm
(suggested)	32–34	34–36	38–40	40–42	44–46	ins.
Actual	93	98	108	113	121.5	cm
measurement	36½	38½	42½	44½	47¾	ins.
Length	78	78	80	82	82	cm
	30¾	30¾	31½	32¼	32¼	ins.
Sleeve length	45	45	45	45	45	cm
	17¾	17¾	17¾	17¾	17¾	ins.

MATERIALS

3 (3, 4, 4, 4) 50g (1¾oz) hanks of Nuna
  in yarn A
3 (3, 4, 4, 4) 50g (1¾oz) hanks of Nuna
  in yarn B
(photographed in: yarn A, Ebony, shade
1001; yarn B, Warm Grey, shade 1002)

NEEDLES

One pair of 3.25mm (US3) knitting needles
One pair of 3mm (US2/3) knitting needles
Knitter's sewing needle or tapestry needle

TENSION (GAUGE)

24 stitches and 34 rows to 10cm (4ins.)
square over pattern using 3.25mm (US3)
needles.

Back and front alike

With 3mm (US2/3) needles and yarn A,
cast on 112 (118, 130, 136, 146) stitches.

RIB PATTERN

Row 1 (right side): K0 (2, 2, 0, 2),
[p2, k2] to end.

Row 2: [P2, k2] to last 0 (2, 2, 0, 2)
stitches, p0 (2, 2, 0, 2).

These 2 rows form the rib pattern.
Repeat the last 2 rows with yarn A only until
work measures 5cm (2ins.) from the
cast-on edge, ending with a right-side row.

MAIN PATTERN

With 3mm (US2/3) needles work rows
1–8 as follows:

Row 1 (wrong side): With yarn A, purl
to end.

Row 2 (right side): With yarn A, knit into
back and front of all stitches.
(224 (236, 260, 272, 292) stitches)

Rows 3, 5, and 7: With yarn A, purl to end.

Rows 4 and 6: With yarn A, knit to end.

Row 8: With yarn A, [k2tog] to end.
(112 (118, 130, 136, 146) stitches)

With 3.25mm (US3) needles work rows
9–14 as follows:

Row 9: With yarn B, purl to end.

Rows 10, 12, and 14: With yarn B, knit to
end.

Rows 11 and 13: With yarn B, purl to end.

These 14 rows form the pattern.
Continue in the pattern until the work
measures approximately 55cm (21½ins.)
from the cast-on edge, ending after row 6
has been completed and with a right-side
row. *(224 (236, 260, 272, 292) stitches)*

SHAPE RAGLANS

Decrease one stitch at each end of next and
8 (8, 6, 6, 1) following 4th rows, then on
following 12 (12, 20, 23, 23) alternate rows.
Work one row in pattern, ending after row
8 (8, 2, 8, 8) has been completed with a
right-side row.
(80 (86, 174, 90, 92) stitches)

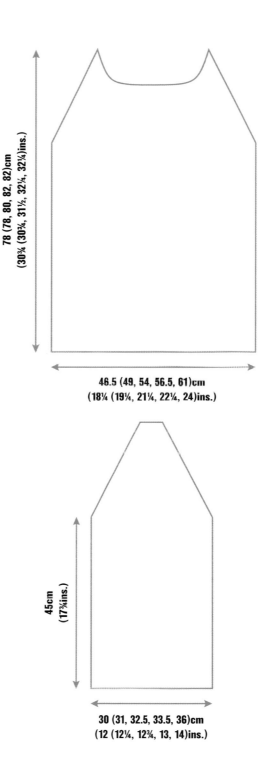

78 (78, 80, 82, 82)cm
(30¾ (30¾, 31½, 32¼, 32¼)ins.)

46.5 (49, 54, 56.5, 61)cm
(18¼ (19¼, 21¼, 22¼, 24)ins.)

45cm
(17¾ins.)

30 (31, 32.5, 33.5, 36)cm
(12 (12¼, 12¾, 13, 14)ins.)

SHAPE RIGHT NECK AND RAGLAN

Next row: P2tog, p13 (13, 25, 13, 13), turn and leave remaining 65 (71, 147, 75, 77) stitches on a stitch holder.

Work one row in pattern.

Decrease one stitch at each end of the next and following 7 alternative rows.

(1, (1, 2, 1, 1,) stitches)

Next row: K1 (1, 0, 1, 1), [k2tog] 0 (0, 1, 0, 0) times.

Fasten off remaining stitch.

With wrong-side facing, leave centre 50 (56, 120, 60, 62) stitches on a stitch holder, rejoin yarn to remaining 15 (15, 27, 15, 15) stitches, purl to the last 2 stitches, p2tog. *(14 (14, 26, 14, 14) stitches)*

Work one row in pattern.

Decrease one stitch at each end of next and following 7 alternative rows.

(1 (1, 2, 1, 1) stitches)

Next row: K1 (1, 0, 1, 1), [k2tog] 0 (0, 1, 0, 0) times.

Fasten off remaining stitch.

Sleeves

With 3mm (US2/3) needles and yarn A, cast on 72 (74, 78, 80, 86) stitches.

Starting with a row 1 of rib pattern for the Back and front, work as given until sleeve measures approximately 45cm (17¾ins.) from the cast-on edge, ending after row 6 of main pattern and with a right-side row.

(144 (148, 156, 160, 172) stitches)

SHAPE RAGLAN

Decrease one stitch at each end of next and 2 (2, 2, 7, 2) following 4th rows, then on following 33 (33, 37, 30, 40) alternate rows.

Work one row in pattern, ending after row 12 (12, 6, 12, 12) of main pattern and with a right-side row.

(16 (18, 32, 20, 18) stitches)

Place the remaining stitches on a stitch holder.

Neck edging

Join raglan seams, leaving front left seam open.

With right side facing, 3mm (US2/3) needles and yarn A, pick up and knit 14 stitches down left front neck, work across 50 (56, 120, 60, 62) stitches from the stitch holder at the front as follows: k50 (56, 0, 60, 62), [k2tog] 0 (0, 60, 0, 0) times, pick up and knit 14 stitches up right front neck, work across 16 (18, 32, 20, 18) stitches from the stitch holder at the top of the right sleeve as follows: k16 (18, 0, 20, 18), [k2tog] 0 (0, 16, 0, 0) times, pick up and knit 14 stitches down right back neck, work across 50 (56, 120, 60, 62) stitches from the stitch holder at the back as follows: k50 (56, 0, 60, 62), [k2tog] 0 (0, 60, 0, 0) times, pick up and knit 14 stitches up left back neck, work across 16 (18, 32, 20, 18) stitches from the stitch holder at the top of the left sleeve as follows: k16 (18, 0, 20, 18), [k2tog] 0 (0, 16, 0, 0) times,

(188 (204, 208, 216, 216) stitches)

Rib row: [K2, p2] to end.

This row forms the rib pattern.

Repeat the last row until neck edging measures 6cm (2¼ins.), ending with a wrong-side row.

Cast (bind) off.

Finishing

Join left raglan and neck edging seam.

Sew together sleeve and side seams.

Weave in ends.

nuna: ruffly-stripes, wide-neck sweater

85

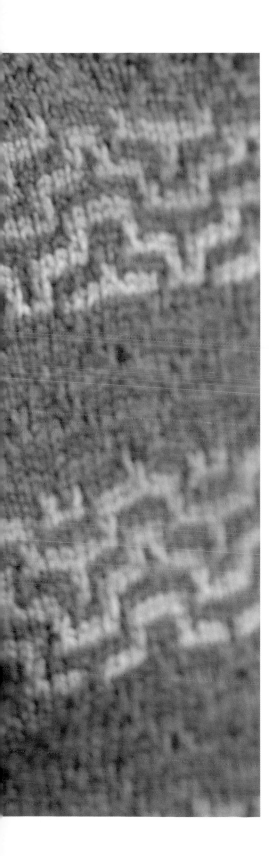

3 Dresses and Tunics

sleeveless dress
page 88

lace, short-sleeved dress
page 92

ribbed, sleeveless tank top
page 96

elongated, v-neck, sleeveless dress
page 100

long, v-necked vest
page 104

SAMP'A
sleeveless dress

The stitch pattern at the top of this dress not only creates a gentle ripple texture in the fabric and beautiful edge detail, but also gives the illusion of separate, small cap sleeves.

MEASUREMENTS

To fit bust	81.5–96.5	101.5–117	cm
(suggested)	32–38	40–46	ins.
Actual	108	131.5	cm
measurement	42½	51¾	ins.
Length	70	70	cm
	27½	27½	ins.

MATERIALS

10 (12) 50g (1¾oz) hanks of Samp'a (photographed in Hickory, shade 608)

NEEDLES

One pair of 3.75mm (US5) knitting needles
Cable needle
One stitch holder
Two markers or safety pins
Knitter's sewing needle or tapestry needle

TENSION (GAUGE)

24 stitches and 32 rows to 10cm (4ins.) square over cable pattern using 3.75mm (US5) needles.

SPECIAL ABBREVIATIONS

T4B: Slip next 2 stitches onto cable needle and hold at back, k2 from left-hand needle, p2 from cable needle.

T4F: Slip next 2 stitches onto cable needle and hold at front, p2 from left-hand needle, k2 from cable needle.

Back and front alike

With 3.75mm (US5) needles, cast on 130 (158) stitches.

RIB PATTERN

Row 1 (right side): P6, k6, *p4, [k2, p4] 3 times, k6, repeat from * to last 6 stitches, p6.

Row 2: K6, p6, [k4, p14, k4, p6] to last 6 stitches, k6.

These 2 rows form the rib pattern.

Repeat the last 2 rows until back measures 45cm (17¾ins.) from the cast-on edge, ending with a wrong-side row.

CABLE PATTERN

Row 1 (right side): P6, k6, *p4, [k2, p4] 3 times, k6, repeat from * to last 6 stitches, p6.

Row 2: K6, p6, [k4, p14, k4, p6] to last 6 stitches, k6.

Row 3: P4, T4B, k2, *[T4F, p2] twice, k2, [p2, T4B] twice, k2, repeat from * to last 8 stitches, T4F, p4.

Row 4: K4, [p10, k4] to end.

Row 5: P2, T4B, p2, k2, *[p2, T4F] twice, k2, [T4B, p2] twice, k2, repeat from * to last 8 stitches, p2, T4F, p2.

Row 6: K2, p14, [k4, p6, k4, p14] to last 2 stitches, k2.

Row 7: P2, *[k2, p4] 3 times, k6, p4, repeat from * to last 16 stitches, k2, [p4, k2] twice, p2.

Row 8: Repeat row 6.

Row 9: P2, T4F, p2, k2, *[p2, T4B] twice, k2, [T4F, p2] twice, k2, repeat from * to last 8 stitches, p2, T4B, p2.

Row 10: Repeat row 4.

Row 11: P4, T4F, k2, *[T4B, p2] twice, k2, [p2, T4F] twice, k2, repeat from * to last 8 stitches, T4B, p4.

Row 12: Repeat row 2

These 12 rows form the cable pattern.

Repeat these last 12 rows until work measures 66cm (26ins.) from the cast-on edge, ending with a wrong-side row. Keeping pattern correct.

SHAPE NECK

Continue keeping pattern correct.

Next row: Work 38 (52) stitches in pattern, place the remaining stitches on a stitch holder, turn.

Work in cable pattern until 12 rows have been worked.

Cast (bind) off.

SHAPE NECK

With right side facing, rejoin yarn to remaining stitches, cast (bind) off centre 54 stitches, work in pattern to end.

Work to match other neck.

Finishing

Join shoulder seams.

Place markers 20cm (7¾ins.) down from shoulder seams and join the side seams beneath markers.

Weave in ends.

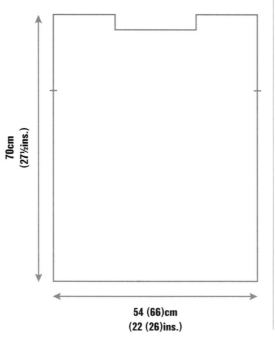

70cm
(27½ins.)

54 (66)cm
(22 (26)ins.)

TUPA
lace, short-sleeved dress

The lace on the top of this dress is a joy. And nothing complements it better than the simplicity of stocking stitch.

MEASUREMENTS

To fit bust						
(suggested)	81.5–86.5	91.5–96.5	101.5–106.5	112–117	117–122	cm
	32–34	36–38	40–42	44–46	46–48	ins.
Actual	94	102	110	118	126	cm
measurement	37	40¼	43¼	46½	49½	ins.
Length	76	76	78	78	80	cm
	30	30	30¾	30¾	31½	ins.
Sleeve length	12	12	12	12	12	cm
	4¾	4¾	4¾	4¾	4¾	ins.

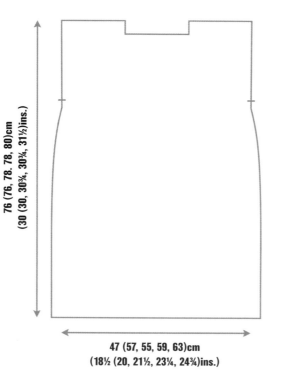

76 (76, 78. 78, 80)cm
(30 (30, 30¾, 30¾, 31½)ins.)

47 (57, 55, 59, 63)cm
(18½ (20, 21½, 23¼, 24¾)ins.)

MATERIALS
8 (9, 9, 10, 10) 50g (1¾oz) hanks of Tupa (photographed in Dark Auburn, shade 810)

NEEDLES
One pair of 3.75mm (US5) knitting needles
One pair of 4mm (US6) knitting needles
Two stitch holders
Two markers or safety pins
Knitter's sewing needle or tapestry needle

TENSION (GAUGE)
20 stitches and 30 rows to 10cm (4ins.) square over lace pattern using 4mm (US6) needles.

22 stitches and 30 rows to 10cm (4ins.) square over stocking (stockinette) stitch using 4mm (US6) needles.

tupa: lace, short-sleeved dress

Back and front alike

With 4mm (US6) needles, cast on
114 (124, 134, 144, 154) stitches.
Starting with a knit row, work in stocking
(stockinette) stitch until work measures
56 (56, 58, 58, 60)cm (22 (22, 22¾,
22¾, 23½)ins.) from the cast-on edge,
ending with a wrong-side row.

Decrease row: K6, [k3, k2tog] to last
8 stitches, k8.
(94 (102, 110, 118, 126) stitches)
Purl one row.

LACE PATTERN

Row 1 (right side): K2, [k2tog, k1, yrn, k1,
sl1, k1, psso, k2] to last 4 stitches, k4.
Row 2 and every alt pattern row: Purl
to end.
Row 3: K1, k2tog, k1, yrn, [k1, yrn, k1,
sl1, k1, psso, k2tog, k1, yrn] to last
2 stitches, k2.
Row 5: K3, yrn, [k3, yrn, k1, sl1, k1, psso,
k1, yrn] to last 3 stitches, k3.
Row 7: K5, [k2tog, k1, yrn, k1,
sl1, k1, psso, k2] to last 2 stitches, k2.
Row 9: K4, *k2tog, k1, [yrn, k1] twice,
sl1, k1, psso, repeat from * to last
3 stitches, k3.
Row 11: K3, k2tog, [k1, yrn, k3, yrn, k1,
k2tog] to last 2 stitches, k2.
Row 12: Purl to end.
These 12 rows form the lace pattern.
Repeat the last 12 rows 3 times.

SHAPE ONE NECK AND SHOULDER

Next row: Work pattern until there are
30 (30, 38, 38, 38) stitches, place
remaining stitches on a stitch holder, turn,
purl to end.
Work 10 rows in pattern.
Cast (bind) off.

SHAPE OTHER NECK AND SHOULDER

With right side facing, leave centre
34 (42, 34, 42, 50) stitches on the stitch
holder, rejoin yarn to 30 (30, 38,
38, 38) stitches.

Work to match one neck and shoulder.
Cast (bind) off.

Sleeves

With 4mm (US6) needles, cast on
78 (86, 86, 94, 94) stitches.
Purl one row.
Starting with a row 1 of lace pattern for the
Back, continue in pattern until sleeve
measures 12cm (4¾ins.) from the cast-on
edge, ending with a wrong-side row.
Cast (bind) off.

Neck edging

Join right shoulder seam.
With right side facing and 3.75mm (US5)
needles, pick up and knit 9 stitches down
left front neck, knit 34 (42, 34, 42, 50)
stitches from stitch holder at front, pick up
and knit 9 stitches up right front neck, pick
up and knit 9 stitches down back neck, pick
up and knit 34 (42, 34, 42, 50) stitches
from stitch holder at back, pick up and knit
9 stitches up back neck.
(104 (120, 104, 120, 136) stitches)
Cast (bind) off on a wrong-side row.

Finishing

Join left shoulder seam and neck edging.
Place markers 20 (21, 21, 23, 23)cm
(7¾ (8¼, 8¼, 9, 9)ins.) down from
shoulder seams.
Sew on sleeves, placing centre of sleeves
to shoulder seams and easing edge
to markers.
Join sleeve seams and side seams beneath
markers.
Weave in ends.

K'ACHA
ribbed, sleeveless tank top

Experimenting with stripe repeats is always fun, and the rib softens the stripe edge and helps to transform the fabric into something unique.

MEASUREMENTS

To fit bust	81.5–86.5	91.5–96.5	96.5–101.5	106.5–112	117–122	cm
	32–34	36–38	38–40	42–44	46–48	ins.
Actual	94	100	105.5	111	116.5	cm
measurement	37	39¼	41½	43¾	45¾	ins.
Length	77	77	79	82	82	cm
	30¼	30¼	31	32¼	32¼	ins.
Sleeve length	45	45	45	45	45	cm
	17¾	17¾	17¾	17¾	17¾	ins.

MATERIALS

2 (3, 3, 4, 4) 50g (1¾oz) hanks each
    of K'acha in yarn A and yarn B
1 (2, 2, 3, 3) 50g (1¾oz) hank (s) each
    of K'acha in yarn C, yarn D, yarn E
    and yarn F
(photographed in: yarn A, Cinnamon, shade
1201; yarn B, Royal Purple, shade 1202;
yarn C, Vintage Green, shade 1207; yarn D,
Deep Navy, shade 1206; yarn E, Magenta
Magic, shade 1204; yarn F, Dark Chocolate,
shade 1205)

NEEDLES

One pair of 3.75mm (US5) knitting needles
One pair of 4mm (US6) knitting needles
One stitch holder
Two markers or safety pins
Knitter's sewing needle or tapestry needle

TENSION (GAUGE)

20 stitches and 26 rows to 10cm (4ins.)
square over rib pattern when slightly
stretched using 4mm (US6) needles.

STRIPE PATTERN

With yarn C, work 1 row.
With yarn D, work 1 row.
With yarn B, work 2 rows.
With yarn E, work 1 row.
With yarn F, work 1 row.
With yarn A, work 2 rows.
With yarn D, work 1 row.
With yarn C, work 1 row.
With yarn B, work 2 rows.
With yarn F, work 1 row.
With yarn E, work 1 row.
With yarn A, work 2 rows.
These 16 rows form the stripe pattern.
Repeat these 16 rows throughout.

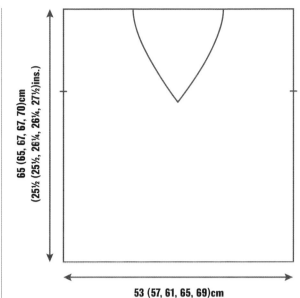

65 (65, 67, 67, 70)cm
(25½ (25½, 26¼, 26¼, 27½)ins.)

53 (57, 61, 65, 69)cm
(21 (22½, 24, 25½, 27)ins.)

Back

With 4mm (US6) needles and yarn A, cast
on 106 (114, 122, 130, 138) stitches.

RIB PATTERN

Row 1 (right side): K2, [p6, k2] to end.
Row 2: P2, [k6, p2] to end.
These 2 rows form the rib pattern.
Starting with the first row of striped pattern,
work in rib pattern and striped pattern until
back measures 65 (65, 67, 67, 70)cm
(25½ (25½, 26¼, 26¼, 27½)ins.) from
the cast-on edge, ending with a wrong-
side row.

SHAPE SHOULDERS

Cast (bind) off 32 (36, 39, 42, 45) stitches
at the beginning of next 2 rows.
Place centre 42 (42, 44, 46, 48) stitches
on a stitch holder.

Front

Work as given for the Back until the front measures 40 (40, 42, 42, 45)cm (15¾ (15¾, 16½, 16½,17¾)ins.) from the cast-on edge, ending with a wrong-side row.

SHAPE LEFT NECK

Next row: Work pattern until there are 53 (57, 61, 65, 69) stitches on right-hand needle, place remaining stitches on a stitch holder, turn.

Next row: K3 (1, 3, 1, 3), p2 (0, 2, 0, 2), [k6, p2] to end.

Decrease row (right side): Work in pattern to last 7 stitches, p2togtbl, k2 (0, 2, 0, 2), p3 (5, 3, 5, 3).

(52 (56, 60, 64, 68) stitches)

This row sets the position of the decrease stitch.

Keeping pattern correct, decrease one stitch at neck edge of every following alternative row until there are 40 (44, 46, 48, 50) stitches.

Work 3 rows in pattern.

Decrease one stitch at neck edge of next and every following 4th row until there are 32 (36, 39, 42, 45) stitches.

Continue without shaping in rib pattern and striped pattern until front measures 65 (65, 67, 67, 70)cm (25½ (25½, 26¼, 26¼, 27½)ins.) from the cast-on edge, ending with a wrong-side row.

Cast (bind) off.

SHAPE RIGHT NECK

With right side facing, rejoin yarn to remaining 53 (57, 61, 65, 69) stitches, work in pattern to end.

Next row: [P2, k6] to last 5 (1, 5, 1, 5) stitches, p2 (1, 2, 1, 2), k3 (0, 3, 0, 3).

Decrease row (right side): P3 (5, 3, 5, 3), k2 (0, 2, 0, 2), p2tog, pattern to end.

(52 (56, 60, 64, 68) stitches)

This row sets the position of the decrease stitch.

Work to match left neck, reversing shaping.

Neck edging

Join right shoulder seam.

With right side facing, 3.75mm (US5) needles and yarn A, pick up and knit 51 stitches down left front neck, pick up and knit 51 stitches up right front neck, pick up and knit 42 (42, 44, 46, 48) stitches from stitch holder at back.

(144 (144, 146, 148, 150) stitches)

Next row: Knit 90 (90, 92, 94, 96) stitches, k2togtbl, k2, k2tog, knit to end.

Cast (bind) off on wrong-side row.

Armhole edging

Join left shoulder and neck edging seam.

Place markers 20 (21, 22, 23, 24)cm (7¾ (8¼, 8¾, 9, 9½)ins.) down from shoulder seams.

With right side facing, 3.75mm (US5) needles and yarn A, pick up and knit 44 (46, 48, 50, 52) stitches from marker up one side of armhole edge, pick up and knit 44 (46, 48, 50, 52) stitches down other side of armhole edge to marker.

(88 (92, 96, 100, 104) stitches)

Knit one row.

Cast (bind) off on wrong-side row.

Finishing

Join the side and armhole edges.

Weave in ends.

k'acha: ribbed, sleeveless tank top

NUNA
elongated, v-neck, sleeveless dress

The combination of this stitch technique and the fine yarn means that this garment can be easily worn over a vest top in summer months too.

MEASUREMENTS

To fit bust (suggested)					
86–91.5	96.5–101.5	106.5–111.5	111.5–116.5	122–127	cm
34–36	38–40	42–44	44–46	48–50	ins.

Actual measurement					
97	106	115	124.5	134	cm
38	41¾	45¼	49	52¾	ins.

Length					
84	84	86	86	88	cm
33	33	33¾	33¾	34½	ins.

MATERIALS

5 (6, 6, 7, 7) 50g (1¾oz) hanks of Nuna
    in yarn A
2 (2, 3, 3, 3) 50g (1¾oz) hanks of Nuna
    in yarn B
(photographed in: yarn A, Maya Blue, shade 1011; yarn B, Myrtle, shade 1010)

NEEDLES

One pair of 3.25mm (US3) knitting needles
One stitch holder
Two markers or safety pins
Knitter's sewing needle or tapestry needle

TENSION (GAUGE)

26 stitches and 32 rows to 10cm (4ins.) square over main pattern using 3.25mm (US3) needles.

Note: The front of this dress uses the intarsia technique. It is the simplest form of intarsia. When joining in the second yarn, twist the two yarns around each other on the wrong side to avoid gaps. The twist is, again, very basic and happens just once by placing the yarn that has just been used over the yarn that is to be used, the yarn to be used is then brought up, thus creating a little twist.

Back

With 3.25mm (US3) needles and yarn A, cast on 126 (138, 150, 162, 174) stitches.
MAIN PATTERN
Row 1 (right side): With yarn A, knit to end.
Row 2: With yarn A, p1, k1, [p5, k1] to last 4 stitches, p4.
These 2 rows form the main pattern.
Repeat the last 2 rows with yarn A only until back measures 40 (40, 41, 42, 42)cm (15¾ (15¾, 16¼, 16½, 16½)ins.) from the cast-on edge, ending with wrong-side row.

RIB PATTERN

Row 1: With yarn B, [k3, p3] to end.
Row 2: With yarn B, [k1, p1] to end.
These 2 rows form the rib pattern.
Repeat the last 2 rows until back measures 48 (48, 49, 50, 50)cm (19 (19, 19¼, 19¾, 19¾)ins.) from the cast-on edge, ending with a wrong-side row.
Starting with row 1 of main pattern and using yarn A only, continue in main pattern until back measures 84 (84, 86, 86, 88)cm (33 (33, 33¾, 33¾ 34½)ins.) from the cast-on edge, ending with a wrong-side row.

SHAPE SHOULDERS

Cast (bind) off 37 (43, 47, 53, 57) stitches at the beginning of next 2 rows.
Cast (bind) off remaining (52 (52, 56, 56, 60) stitches)

Front

Work as given for the back until front measures 48 (48, 49, 50, 50)cm (19 (19, 19¼, 19¾, 19¾)ins.) from the cast-on edge, ending with a wrong-side row.

SHAPE LEFT NECK

Next row: With yarn A, k39 (45, 51, 57, 63), with yarn B, work 24 stitches in pattern, place remaining stitches on a stitch holder, turn.
Next row (wrong side): With yarn B, pattern 24 stitches, with yarn A, purl to end.
Next row (right side): With yarn A, knit to last 24 stitches, with yarn B, work in pattern to end.
These 2 rows set the position of the ribbing. Work one row in pattern.
Decrease row (right side): With yarn A, knit to last 26 stitches, k2togtbl, with yarn B, work in pattern to end.
Decrease one stitch as set above at neck edge of next and every following 4th row until there are 37 (43, 47, 53, 57) stitches.

Continue without shaping in pattern until front measures 84 (84, 86, 86, 88)cm (33 (33, 33¾, 33¾, 34½)ins.) from the cast-on edge, ending with a wrong-side row. Cast (bind) off.

SHAPE RIGHT NECK

With right side facing, rejoin yarn to remaining 63 (69, 75, 81, 87) stitches, with yarn B, work in pattern for 24 stitches, with yarn A, knit to end. Work to match left neck, reversing shaping.

Armhole edging

Join shoulder seams.

Place markers 20 (21, 22, 23, 24)cm (7¾ (8¼, 8¾, 9, 9½)ins.) down from shoulder seams.

With right side facing, 3.25mm (US 3) needles and yarn B, pick up and knit 48 (51, 54, 57, 60) stitches from marker up one side of armhole edge, pick up and knit 48 (51, 54, 57, 60) stitches down other side of armhole edge to marker. *(96 (102, 108, 114, 120) stitches)*

RIB PATTERN

Row 1 (wrong side): [K1, p1] to end.

Row 2: [K3, p3] to end.

Work the rib row 1 once more.

Cast (bind) off in rib pattern.

Finishing

Join the side and armhole edging seams.

Weave in ends.

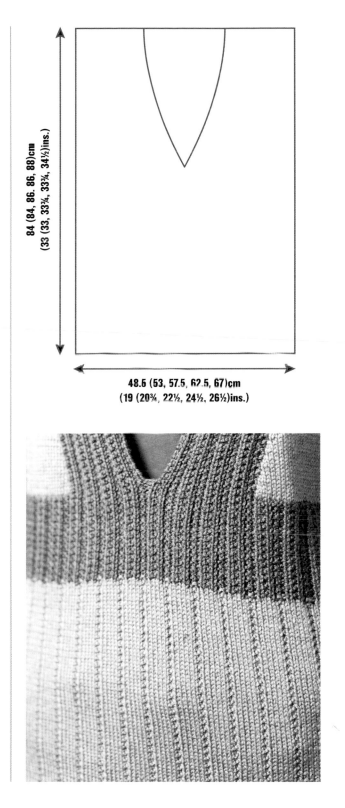

84 (84, 86, 86, 88)cm (33 (33, 33¾, 33¾, 34½)ins.)

48.5 (53, 57.5, 62.5, 67)cm (19 (20¾, 22½, 24½, 26½)ins.)

NUNA
long, v-necked vest

This vest has so many elements to enjoy. Both the slip stitch technique and the striping are simple to do but create a fabric that looks more complicated.

MEASUREMENTS

To fit bust	76.5–81.5	81.5–86.5	91.5–96.5	101.5–106.5	106.5–112	cm
	30–32	32–34	36–38	40–42	42–44	ins.
Actual	81	90	98.5	107	115.5	cm
measurement	31¾	35¼	38¾	42¼	45¼	ins.
Length	60	60	62	66	66	cm
	23½	23½	24½	26	26	ins.
Sleeve	6	6	6	6	6	cm
length	2¼	2¼	2¼	2¼	2¼	ins.

MATERIALS

3 (4, 4, 5, 5) 50g (1¾oz) hanks of Nuna
    in yarn A

1 (2, 2, 2, 3) 50g (1¾oz) hanks of Nuna
    in yarn B

1 (2, 2, 3, 3) 50g (1¾oz) hanks of Nuna
    in yarn C

1 (1, 1, 2, 2) 50g (1¾oz) hank(s) of Nuna
    in yarn D

(photographed in: yarn A, Prussian Blue,
shade 1005; yarn B, Ocean Blue, shade
1008; yarn C, Cardinal Red, shade 1004;
yarn D, Maya Blue, shade 1011)

NEEDLES

One pair of 3mm (US2/3) knitting needles
One pair of 3.25mm (US3) knitting needles
Two stitch holders
Knitter's sewing needle or tapestry needle

TENSION (GAUGE)

25 stitches and 32 rows to 10cm (4ins.)
square over pattern using 3.25mm (US3)
needles.

STRIPE PATTERN

With yarn A, work 2 rows.
With yarn B, work 2 rows.
With yarn A, work 2 rows.
With yarn B, work 2 rows.
With yarn A, work 2 rows.
With yarn B, work 2 rows.
With yarn A, work 2 rows.
With yarn C, work 2 rows.
With yarn A, work 2 rows.
With yarn C, work 2 rows.
With yarn A, work 2 rows.
With yarn C, work 2 rows.
With yarn A, work 2 rows.
With yarn C, work 2 rows.
With yarn A, work 2 rows.
With yarn D, work 2 rows.
With yarn A, work 2 rows.
With yarn D, work 2 rows.

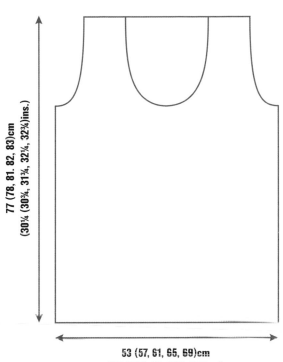

77 (78, 81, 82, 83)cm
(30¼ (30¾, 31¾, 32¼, 32¾)ins.)

53 (57, 61, 65, 69)cm
(21 (22½, 24, 25½, 27)ins)

105

Back

With 3mm (US2/3) needles with yarn A, cast on 124 (136, 148, 160, 172) stitches.

RIB PATTERN

Row 1: [P2, k2] to end.

This row forms the rib patt.

Repeat the last row with yarn A only until back measures 10cm (4ins.) from the cast-on edge, ending with right-side row. Purl one row, increase one stitch in the centre of the row.

(125 (137, 149, 161, 173) stitches)

Change to 3.25mm (US3) needles. Starting with row 1 of the stripe pattern, work stripe pattern throughout:

SLIP STITCH PATTERN

Row 1 (right side): K4, [sl1, k7, sl1, k3] to last stitch, k1.

Row 2: P4, [sl1, p7, sl1, p3] to last stitch, p1.

Row 3: K5, [sl1, k5] to end.

Row 4: P5, [sl1, p5] to end.

Row 5: K6, sl1, k3, sl1, [k7, sl1, k3, s1] to last 6 stitches, k6.

Row 6: P6, sl1, p3, sl1, [p7, sl1, p3, s1] to last 6 stitches, p6.

Row 7: K2, sl1, k4, sl1, k1, sl1, *[k4, s1] twice, k1, s1; repeat from * to last 7 stitches, k4, sl1, k2.

Row 8: P2, sl1, p4, sl1, p1, sl1, *[p4, s1] twice, p1, s1; repeat from * to last 7 stitches, p4, sl1, p2.

Row 9: [K1, s1] twice, *[k4, s1] twice, k1, s1; repeat from * to last stitch, k1.

Row 10: [P1, s1] twice, *[p4, s1] twice, p1, s1; repeat from * to last stitch, p1.

These 10 rows form the slip stitch pattern. Repeat these 10 rows with the striped pattern until back measures 55 (56, 57, 58, 59)cm (21½, 22, 22½, 22¾, 23¼)ins.) from the cast-on edge, ending with a wrong-side row.

SHAPE ARMHOLES

Cast (bind) off 5 stitches at the beginning of the next 2 rows.

(115 (127, 139, 151, 163) stitches)

Decrease row: Work 3 stitches in pattern, sl1, k1, psso, work in pattern to last 5 stitches, k2tog, work in pattern to the end.

(113 (125, 137, 149, 161) stitches)

This row sets the position of the decrease. Decrease one stitch as set above at each end of 6 following alternate rows.

(101 (113, 125, 137, 149) stitches)

Decrease one stitch as set above at each end of 6 following 4th rows.

(89 (101, 113, 125, 137) stitches)

Continue without shaping in slip stitch pattern and striped pattern until armhole measures 22 (22, 24, 24, 24)cm (8¾ (8¾, 9½, 9½, 9½)ins.) from start of armhole shaping, ending with a wrong side row.

SHAPE SHOULDERS

Cast (bind) off 19 (24, 29, 34, 39) stitches at the beginning of next 2 rows. Place remaining 51 (53, 55, 57, 59) stitches on a stitch holder.

Front

Work as given for the Back until the shape armholes, ending with a wrong-side row.

(125 (137, 149, 161, 173) stitches)

SHAPE LEFT NECK AND ARMHOLE

Next row: Cast (bind) off 5 stitches, work in pattern until there are 45 (50, 55, 60, 65) stitches on right-hand needle, place remaining stitches on a stitch holder, turn. Work one row in pattern.

Decrease one stitch at position set for back at each end of next and 6 following alternate rows. *(31 (36, 41, 46, 51) stitches)*

Work 3 rows in pattern.

Decrease one stitch at each end of next and 5 following 4th rows.

(19 (24, 29, 34, 39) stitches)

Continue without shaping in slip stitch pattern and striped pattern until armhole measures 22 (22, 24, 24, 24)cm (8¾ (8¾, 9½, 9½, 9½)ins.) from start of armhole shaping, ending with a wrong-side row.

Cast (bind) off.

SHAPE RIGHT NECK AND ARMHOLE

With right side facing, leave centre 25 (27, 29, 31, 33) stitches on the stitch holder, rejoin yarn to remaining 50 (55, 60, 65, 70) stitches, work in pattern to end.

Cast (bind) off 5 stitches at the beginning of the next row.

Work to match left neck and armhole.

Neck edging

Join right shoulder seam.

With right side facing, 3mm (US2/3) needles and yarn A, pick up and knit 72 (72, 76, 76, 76) stitches down left front neck, knit 25 (27, 29, 31, 33) stitches from stitch holder at front increasing or decreasing one stitch evenly to make 26 (26, 30, 30, 34) stitches at centre front, pick up and knit 73 (73, 77, 77, 77) stitches up right front neck and pick up and knit 51 (53, 55, 57, 59) stitches from stitch holder at back.

(222 (224, 238, 240, 246) stitches)

RIB PATTERN

Row 1 (wrong side): P2 (0, 2, 0, 2), [k2, p2] 30 (31, 32, 33, 33) times, k4, p2, [k2, p2] 5 (5, 6, 6, 7) times, k4, [p2, k2] to last 2 (0, 2, 0, 2) stitches, p2.

This row sets the rib patt.

Row 2: Rib to p4, p2tog, rib to next p4 then, p2, p2togtbl, rib to end.

Row 3: Rib to k3, k2togtbl, rib to next k3 then, k1, k2tog, rib to end.

Cast (bind) off in rib.

Armhole edging

Join left shoulder and neck edging seam.

With right side facing, 3mm (US2/3) needles and yarn A, pick up and knit 77 (77, 81, 81, 81) stitches up one side of armhole edge, pick up and knit 77 (77, 81, 81, 81) stitches down other side of armhole.

(154 (154, 162, 162, 162) stitches)

RIB PATTERN

Row 1 (wrong side): P2, [k2, p2] to end.

Row 2: K2, [p2, k2] to end.

Repeat row 1 of rib once more.

Cast (bind) off in rib.

Finishing

Join the side and armhole seams.

Weave in ends.

nuna: long, v-necked vest

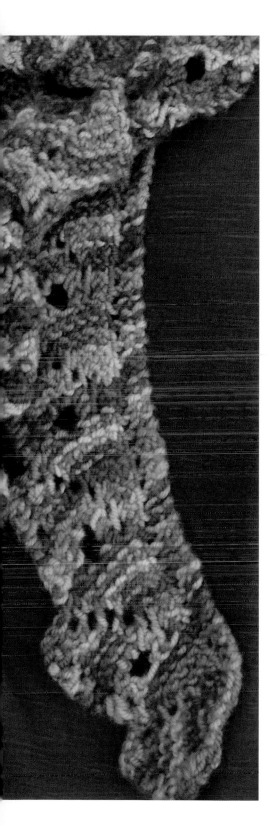

4

Hats, Scarves and Mittens

slouchy socks
page 112

extra long chunky scarf
page 114

moss stitch floppy hat
page 116

mock-cable beret
page 118

mittens with finger cover-flap
page 120

fingerless gloves
page 124

skinny lace scarf
page 126

TUPA

slouchy socks

These socks have a cosy feel. Knitted socks that are a little bit too big for the foot are perfect for lazing around in at home.

SIZE
To fit shoe size UK 4–7 (US 6–9)

MATERIALS
Three 50g (1¾oz) hanks of Tupa (photographed in Electrical Purple, shade 814)

NEEDLES
Set of 4 double pointed 4mm (US6) knitting needles
Cable needle
Knitter's sewing needle or tapestry needle

TENSION (GAUGE)
22 stitches and 28 rows to 10cm (4ins.) square over pattern using 4mm (US6) needles.

SPECIAL ABBREVIATIONS
C4F: Slip next 2 stitches onto cable needle and hold at front, k2 from left-hand needle, k2 from cable needle.

Socks
With 4mm (US6) needles cast on 60 stitches. Distribute stitches evenly onto 3 needles as follows: needle one, 20 stitches; needle two, 20 stitches; needle three, 20 stitches.
(20–20–20 stitches)

RIB PATTERN
Rib round: [K2, p2] twice, *k2, p3, [k2, p2] twice, repeat from * to end.

This round forms the rib pattern.

MAIN PATTERN
Round 1: K2, p1, C4F, p1, [k1, yrn, sl1, k1, psso, k1, k2tog, yrn, k1, p1, C4F, p1] to end.
Rounds 2 and 4: K2, [p1, k4, p1, k7] to last 6 stitches, p1, k4, p1.
Round 3: K2, p1, k4, p1, [k2, yrn, sl1, k2tog, psso, yrn, k2, p1, k4, p1] to end.
These 4 rounds form the pattern.
Repeat the last 4 rounds until sock measures 30cm (12ins.) from the cast-on edge, ending with either round 2 or 4 of main pattern.
Work in rib pattern for 4 rounds.

SHAPE HEEL
Rearrange stitches for the heel as follows: needle one, knit 15 stitches; needle three, slip last 15 stitches onto end of first needle. These 30 stitches are for the heel. Leave the remaining stitches on the two needles for instep.
Keeping rib pattern correct, continue in rib pattern until 21 rows have been worked, ending with a wrong-side row.
Next row: K19, k2tog, turn.
Next row (wrong side): P10, p2tog, turn.
Next row (right side): K10, k2tog, turn.
Repeat the last 2 rows 4 times more, ending with a right-side row.
Next row (wrong side): P10, p2tog, turn.
(18 stitches)
Next row: K6.

Slip remaining 30 stitches for instep onto one needle.

Rearrange stitches as follows: needle one, work remaining 9 stitches of heel in pattern, then pick up and knit 12 stitches along side of heel; needle two, work main pattern across 30 instep stitches; needle three, pick up and knit 12 stitches along other side of heel and remaining 9 stitches of heel. *(21–30–21 stitches)*

SHAPE INSTEP

Next round: Work in pattern.

Next round: Needle one, work in pattern to last 3 stitches, k2tog, k1; needle two, work in pattern; needle 3, k1, k2togtbl, work in pattern to end ot needle.

Repeat the last 2 rounds until 60 stitches remain. *(15–30–15 stitches)*

Starting with a round 1 of rib pattern continue without shaping in rib pattern until foot measures 16cm (6¼ins.) (or desired length) from the start of heel shaping

SHAPE TOE

Next round: Needle one, work in pattern to last 3 stitches, k2tog, k1; needle two, k1, k2togtbl, work in pattern to last 3 stitches on second needle, k2tog, k1; needle three, k1, k2togtbl, work in pattern to end of needle.

Repeat this round until 20 stitches remain. *(5–10–5 stitches)*

Work in pattern for 1 round.

Knit 5 stitches from first needle and slip 5 stitches from third needle onto end of first needle.

Graft (Kitchener stitch) stitches together.

For second sock, repeat from cast on.

Finishing

Weave in ends.

SULKA
extra long chunky scarf

In cold winter months it is lovely to wrap up with an extra long chunky scarf, and the Sulka yarns are such fun to knit with that the knitting of the scarf is just as pleasurable as the wearing of the scarf.

MEASUREMENTS
23 x 245cm (9ins. x 96¼ins.)

MATERIALS
Twelve 50g (1¾oz) hanks of Sulka (photographed in Marshmallow, shade 213)

NEEDLES
One pair of 6mm (US10) knitting needles
Cable needle
Knitter's sewing needle or tapestry needle

TENSION (GAUGE)
18 stitches and 22 rows to 10cm (4ins.) square over pattern using 6mm (US10) needles.

SPECIAL ABBREVIATIONS
C4B: Slip next 2 stitches onto cable needle and hold at back, k2 from left-hand needle, k2 from cable needle.
C4F: Slip next 2 stitches onto cable needle and hold at front, k2 from left-hand needle, k2 from cable needle.

Scarf

With 6mm (US10) needles, cast on 42 stitches.

RIB PATTERN
Row 1 (right side): P2, [k3, p2] to end.
Row 2: K2, [p3, k2] to end.
Repeat the last 2 rows once more.

CABLE PATTERN
Row 1 (right side): P2, [k4, C4F, p2] to end.
Row 2 and every alternate row: K2, [p8, k2] to end.
Row 3: P2, [k8, p2] to end.
Row 5: Repeat row 1.
Row 7: P2, [C4B, k4, p2] to end.
Row 9: Repeat row 3.
Row 11: Repeat row 7.
Row 12: K2, [p8, k2] to end
These 12 rows form the cable pattern.
Repeat the last 12 rows until work measures 243cm (95½ins.) from the cast-on edge, ending with a wrong-side row.
Starting with a row 1 of rib pattern, work 4 rows in rib.
Cast (bind) off.

Finishing
Weave in ends.

SULKA
moss stitch floppy hat

Nothing is as comfortable as a warm head, and nothing beats the warmth of the Sulka yarn. The floppy nature of the hat means that it isn't too tight on your head and is easy to wear.

MEASUREMENTS
Circumference: 50cm (19¾ins.)

MATERIALS
Three 50g (1¾oz) hanks of Sulka (photographed in Wine, shade 203)

NEEDLES
One pair of 5mm (US8) knitting needles
One pair of 6mm (US10) knitting needles
Knitter's sewing needle or tapestry needle

TENSION (GAUGE)
14 stitches and 26 rows to 10cm (4ins.) square over moss (seed) stitch using 6mm (US10) needles.

Hat
With 5mm (US8) needles, cast on 70 stitches.
RIB PATTERN
Row 1 (right side): K2, [p2, k2] to end.
Row 2: P2, [k2, p2] to end.
Repeat the last 2 rows once more.
Change to 6mm (US10) needles.
MAIN PATTERN
Row 1: [K1, p1] to end.
Row 2: [P1, k1] to end.
These 2 rows form the moss (seed) stitch pattern.

Repeat the last 2 rows until hat measures 20cm (7¾ins.) from the cast-on edge, ending with a wrong-side row.
SHAPE CROWN
Row 1 (right side): K1, p1, [k2tog, k1, p1] to end. *(53 stitches)*
Row 2: P1, [k2, p1] to last stitch, k1.
Row 3: K1, p1, [k2tog, p1] to end. *(36 stitches)*
Row 4: [P1, k1] to end.
Row 5: [K1, p1, k2tog, k1, p1] to end. *(30 stitches)*
Row 6: [P1, k2, p1, k1] to end.
Row 7: [K1, p1, k2tog, p1] to end. *(24 stitches)*
Row 8: [P1, k1] to end.
Row 9: [K2tog] to end. *(12 stitches)*
Row 10: [P2tog] to end. *(6 stitches)*
Break off yarn. Thread through 6 stitches.
Pull securely and fasten off.

Finishing
Sew up back seam.
Weave in ends.

mock-cable beret

A beret is a classic, a perennial that takes any fashion trend and makes it individual. The mock-cable pattern enhances the decreases around the crown as well as creating an interesting texture to knit.

MEASUREMENTS
Circumference: 49cm (19¼ins.)

MATERIALS
Two 50g (1¾oz) hanks of K'acha.
(photographed in Kingfisher Blue, shade 1203)

NEEDLES
One pair of 4mm (US6) knitting needles
Cable needle
Knitter's sewing needle or tapestry needle

TENSION (GAUGE)
20 stitches and 26 rows to 10cm (4ins.)
square over stocking (stockinette) stitch
using 4mm (US6) needles.

SPECIAL ABBREVIATIONS
C3B: Slip next 2 stitches onto a cable needle
and hold at back of work, knit next stitch
from left-hand needle, then knit stitches from
cable needle.
C3F: Slip next stitch onto a cable needle and
hold at front of work, knit next 2 stitches
from left-hand needle, then knit stitch from
cable needle.

Hat
With 4mm (US6) needles, cast on
98 stitches.
RIB PATTERN
Row 1 (wrong side): K2, [p2, k2] to end.
Row 2: P2, [k2, p2] to end.
Repeat the last 2 rows once more.
CABLE PATTERN
Row 1 (wrong side): K2, [p6, k2] to end.
Row 2: P2, [k2, sl2, k2, p1, m1, p1] to last
8 stitches, k2, sl2, k2, p2. *(109 stitches)*
Row 3: K2, [p2, sl2, p2, k3] to last
8 stitches, p2, sl2, p2, k2.
Row 4: P2, [C3B, C3F, p3] to last
8 stitches, C3B, C3F, p2.
Row 5: K2, [p6, k3] to last 8 stitches,
p6, k2.
Row 6: P2, [k2, sl2, k2, p2, m1, p1] to last
8 stitches, k2, sl2, k2, p2. *(120 stitches)*
Row 7: K2, [p2, sl2, p2, k4] to last
8 stitches, p2, sl2, p2, k2.
Row 8: P2, [C3B, C3F, p4] to last
8 stitches, C3B, C3F, p2.
Row 9: K2, [p6, k4] to last 8 stitches,
p6, k2.
Row 10: P2, [k2, sl2, k2, p2, m1, p2] to
last 8 stitches, k2, sl2, k2, p2.
(131 stitches)

These rows set the position of the increases and cable patterning.

Keeping pattern correct, continue to increase in this way on every following alternate row until there are 186 stitches, ending with a right-side row.

Work 7 rows in pattern.

SHAPE CROWN

Decrease row (right side): P2, [k2, sl2, k2, p2tog, p8] to last 8 stitches, k2, sl2, k2, p2. *(175 stitches)*

This row sets the position of the decrease stitches, continue to decrease in this way on every 4th row until there are 98 stitches.

Work 3 rows in pattern.

Next row: P2, [slip next 2 stitches onto a cable needle and hold at back of work, knit next stitch from left hand needle, then k2tog from cable needle, slip next stitch onto a cable needle and hold at front of work, k2tog from left hand needle, then knit stitch from cable needle, p2] to end. *(74 stitches)*

Work 3 rows in pattern.

Next row: P2, [k2tog, sl1, k1, psso, p2] to end. *(50 stitches)*

Work 5 rows in pattern.

Next row: P2tog, [k2tog, p2tog] to end. *(25 stitches)*

Work one row in pattern.

Next row: [K2tog] to last stitch, k1. *(13 stitches)*

Next row: [P2tog] to last stitch, p1. *(7 stitches)*

Break off yarn. Thread through 7 stitches. Pull securely and fasten off.

Finishing

Sew back seam together.

Weave in ends.

AKAPANA
mittens with finger cover-flap

In the cold, winter months cosy, snug hands make all the difference, however, when you have to take gloves or mittens off, they are easily misplaced. This is my solution – fingerless mittens with a finger cover.

SIZE
To fit small to average-sized hand

MATERIALS
Two 50g (1¾oz) hanks of Akapana (photographed in Navy Brights, shade 1308)

NEEDLES
Set of 4 double pointed 4mm (US6)
    knitting needles
Two stitch holders
Knitter's sewing needle or tapestry needle

TENSION (GAUGE)
22 stitches and 26 rows to 10cm (4ins.) square over pattern using 4mm (US6) needles.

Rib edging (make two)
With 4mm (US6) needles, cast on 18 stitches.
RIB PATTERN
Row 1: P2, [k2, p2] to end.
Row 2: K2, [p2, k2] to end.
Repeat the last 2 rows until 8 rows have been worked.
Leave stitches on a stitch holder.

First mitten
With 4mm (US6) needles, cast on 36 stitches. Distribute stitches evenly onto three needles as follows: needle one, 12 stitches; needle two, 12 stitches; needle three, 12 stitches. (12–12–12 stitches)
Work in rounds as follows:
Round 1: [K2, p2] to end.
Repeat the last 2 rounds until mitten measures 12cm (4¾ins.) from the cast-on edge.
Shape thumb in stocking (stockinette) stitch as follows:
SHAPE THUMB
Next round: Needle one, k6, m1, k1, m1; needles two and three, knit to end.
(14–12–12 stitches)
Knit 3 rounds.

Next round: Needle one, k6, m1, k3, m1; needles two and three, knit to end. *(16–12–12 stitches)*

Knit 3 rounds.

Next round: Needle one, k6, m1, k5, m1; needles two and three, knit to end. *(18–12–12 stitches)*

Knit one round.

WORK THUMB

Next round: Needle one, k14, turn and slip first 4 stitches onto third needle. Slip remaining 4 stitches on first needle onto second needle.

Working in rows on these 10 stitches only, cast on 2 stitches, knit to end. *(12 stitches)*

Work 7 rows in stocking (stockinette) stitch.

Next row: [K2tog] to end. *(6 stitches)*

Next row: [P2tog] to end. *(3 stitches)*

Break off yarn. Thread through 3 stitches. Pull securely and fasten off.

WORK HAND

Rearrange the stitches as follows; needle one (one of the two spare needles), slip 4 stitches from needle three (the needle to the right of the thumb), with wrong sides of thumb together, rejoin yarn, with needle one starting from edge, pick up and knit 4 stitches along the cast-on edge of thumb, knit 4 stitches from second needle (needle to the left of the thumb); needle two, knit 12 stitches; needle three, knit 12 stitches. *(12–12–12 stitches)*

Next round: Needle one, k6, p2, k2, p2; needle two, [k2, p2] to end; needle three, knit to end.

Repeat the last round 7 times more.

Next round: Needle one, k6, cast (bind) off remaining 6 stitches; needle two, cast (bind) off all 12 stitches; needle three, knit to end.

Next round: Needle one, k6, pick up and knit 6 stitches from rib edging on stitch holder; needle two, pick up and knit 12 stitches from rib edging on stitch holder;

needle three, knit to end.

Starting with a knit round, continue in stocking (stockinette) stitch until top measures 7cm (2¾ins.) from base of thumb seam.

SHAPE TOP

Next round: Needle one, k4, k2togtbl, k2tog, k4; needle two, knit to last 2 stitches, k2togtbl; needle three, k2tog, knit to end.

Next round: Needle one, k3, k2togtbl, k2tog, k3; needle two, knit to last 2 stitches, k2togtbl; needle three, k2tog, knit to end.

Next round: Needle one, k2, k2togtbl, k2tog, k2; needle two, knit to last 2 stitches, k2togtbl; needle three, k2tog, knit to end.

Next round: Needle one, k1, k2togtbl, k2tog, k1; needle two, knit to last 2 stitches, k2togtbl; needle three, k2tog, knit to end.

Next round: Needle one, k2togtbl, k2tog; needle two, knit to last 2 stitches, k2togtbl; needle three, k2tog, knit to end.

(2–7–7 stitches)

Knit one round.

Slip stitch from first needle onto the third needle then slip remaining stitch on first needle onto second needle.

Graft (Kitchener stitch) stitches together.

Second mitten

Work as given for first mitten until Work thumb.

Next round: Needle one, k14, turn and slip first 4 of these stitches onto third needle. Slip remaining 4 stitches on first needle onto second needle.

Working in rows on these 10 stitches only, purl 10 stitches, turn and cast on 2 stitches. *(12 stitches)*

Work 6 rows in stocking (stockinette) stitch.

Next row: [K2tog] to end. *(6 stitches)*

Next row: [P2tog] to end. *(3 stitches)*

Break off yarn. Thread through 3 stitches. Pull securely and fasten off.

WORK HAND

Rearrange the stitches as follows; needle one, slip last 4 stitches from third needle onto needle one, with wrong sides of thumb together, rejoin yarn, pick up 4 stitches along the cast-on edge of thumb, knit 4 stitches from needle two; needle two, knit 12 stitches; needle three, knit 12 stitches. *(12–12–12 stitches)*

Next round: Needle one, p2, k2, p2, k6 on first needle; needle two, knit to end; needle three, [k2, p2] to end. Repeat the last round 7 times more.

Next round: Needle one, p2, k2, p2, k6; needle two, knit to end; needle three, cast (bind) off 12 stitches.

Next round: Needle one, cast (bind) off 6 stitches, knit to end; needle two, knit to end; needle three, pick up and knit 12 stitches from rib edging on stitch holder.

Next round: Needle one, pick up and knit remaining 6 stitches from rib edging on stitch holder, k6, needle two, knit to end; needle three, knit to end.

Starting with a knit round, continue in stocking (stockinette) stitch until top measures 7cm (2¾ins.) from base of thumb seam.

Complete as given for first mitten from Shape top.

Finishing

Join thumb seams.

Weave in ends.

K'ACHA
fingerless gloves

These fingerless gloves are a joy to wear and the stitch pattern is simply the reverse side of single-row stripes, worked in three shades, in stocking stitch.

SIZE
To fit small to average-sized hand

MATERIALS
One 50g (1¾oz) hank of K'acha in yarn A,
    yarn B, and yarn C
(photographed in: yarn A, Deep Navy, shade
1206; yarn B, Kingfisher Blue, shade 1203;
yarn C, Dark Chocolate, shade 1205)

NEEDLES
Set of 4 double pointed 4mm (US6)
    knitting needles
Knitter's sewing needle or tapestry needle

TENSION (GAUGE)
20 stitches and 30 rows to 10cm (4ins.)
square over pattern using 4mm (US6)
needles.

First mitten
With 4mm (US6) needles and yarn A, cast
on 36 stitches. Distribute stitches evenly
onto 3 needles as follows: needle one,
12 stitches; needle two, 12 stitches; needle
three, 12 stitches. *(12–12–12 stitches)*
Work in rounds as follows:
STRIPE PATTERN
Round 1 (wrong side): With yarn B, knit.
Round 2: With yarn C, knit to end.
Round 3: With yarn A, knit to end.
These 3 rounds form the 3 stripe pattern.

Repeat throughout.
Continue in stripe pattern until work measures
12cm (4¾ins.) from the cast-on edge.
SHAPE THUMB
Next round: Needle one, k6, m1, k1, m1;
needles two and three, knit to end.
(14–12–12 stitches)
Knit 3 rounds.
Next round: Needle one, k6, m1, k3, m1;
needles two and three, knit to end.
(16–12–12 stitches)
Knit 3 rounds.
Next round: Needle one, k6, m1, k5, m1;
needles two and three, knit to end.
(18–12–12 stitches)
Knit one round.
WORK THUMB
Next round: Needle one, k14, turn and slip
first 4 of these stitches onto third needle. Slip
remaining 4 stitches on first needle onto
second needle.
Working in rows on these 10 stitches only,
cast on 3 stitches. *(13 stitches)*
Work 8 rows in stripe pattern.
Cast (bind) off.
WORK HAND
Working in the stripe pattern, rearrange
the stitches as follows; needle one (one of
the two spare needles), slip 4 stitches from
needle three (the needle to the right of the
thumb), with wrong sides of thumb together,
rejoin yarn, with needle one starting from
edge, pick up and knit 4 stitches along the

cast-on edge of thumb, knit 4 stitches from second needle (needle to the left of the thumb); needle two, knit 12 stitches; needle three, knit 12 stitches.

(12–12–12 stitches)

Continue in pattern until top measures 5cm (2ins.).

Cast (bind) off.

Second mitten

Work as given for first mitten until Work thumb.

WORK THUMB

Next round: Needles one and two, knit to end; needle three, k14, turn and slip first 4 stitches of third needle onto second needle. Slip remaining 4 stitches on third needle onto first needle.

Working in rows on these 10 stitches only, cast on 3 stitches. *(13 stitches)*

Work 8 rows in stripe pattern.

Cast (bind) off.

WORK HAND

Working in the stripe pattern, rearrange the stitches as follows; needle three (one of the two spare needles), slip last 4 stitches from needle two (the needle to the right of the thumb), with wrong sides of thumb together, rejoin yarn, with needle three, starting from edge, pick up and knit 4 stitches along the cast-on edge of thumb, then, knit 4 stitches from first needle (the needle to the left of the thumb); needle two, knit 12 stitches; needle one, knit 12 stitches.

(12–12–12 stitches)

Continue in pattern until top measures 5cm (2ins.).

Cast (bind) off.

Finishing

Join thumb seams.

Weave in ends.

HACHO
skinny lace scarf

This is an easy weekend knit to create a beautiful knitted accessory that heightens any garment. To make your skinny scarf twinkle you can add beads or sequins to your scarf.

MEASUREMENTS
6.5 x 200cm (2½ins. x 78¾ins.) approx.

MATERIALS
Two 50g (1¾oz) hanks of Hachoor or Tupa for a single shade alternative (photographed in Sapphire Jade, shade 304)

NEEDLES
One pair of 4mm (US6) knitting needles. Knitter's sewing needle or tapestry needle

TENSION (GAUGE)
10 stitches to 6.5cm (2½ins.) and 34 rows to 10cm (4ins.) square over pattern using 4mm (US6) needles.

Scarf
With 4mm (US6) needles, cast on 10 stitches.
Knit one row.

MAIN PATTTERN
Row 1: Sl1, k1, [yrn, k2tog] twice, [yrn] 4 times, k2tog, yrn, p2tog.
Row 2: Yrn, p2tog, k1, [k1, p1] twice into the large yrn loop, [k1, p1] twice, k2.
Row 3: Sl1, [k1, yrn, k2tog] twice, k4, yrn, p2tog.
Row 4: Yrn, p2tog, k5, [p1, k2] twice.
Row 5: Sl1, k1, yrn, k2tog, k2, yrn, k2tog, k3, yrn, p2tog.

Row 6: Yrn, p2tog, k4, p1, k3, p1, k2.
Row 7: Sl1, k1, yrn, k2tog, k3, yrn, k2tog, k2, yrn, p2tog.
Row 8: Yrn, p2tog, k3, p1, k4, p1, k2.
Row 9: Sl1, k1, yrn, k2tog, k4, yrn, k2tog, k1, yrn, p2tog.
Row 10: Yrn, p2tog, k2, p1, k5, p1, k2.
Row 11: Sl1, k1, yrn, k2tog, k5, yrn, k2tog, yrn, p2tog.
Row 12: Cast (bind) off 3 stitches, then slip the stitch from right-hand needle back onto left-hand needle, yrn, p2tog, k5, p1, k2.
These 12 rows form the pattern.
Repeat the last 12 rows until scarf measures 200cm (78¾ins.) from the cast-on edge, (or keep knitting until both hanks are used up) ending with row 12 of the pattern.
Knit one row.
Cast (bind) off.

Finishing
Weave in ends.

distributors

USA
Knitting Fever Inc
315 Bayview Ave,
Amityville,
New York11701
Tel: (+516) 546 3600
Fax: (+516) 546 6871
www.knittingfever.com

CANADA
Diamond Yarn Ltd
155 Martin Ross Avenue,
Unit 3, Toronto,
Ontario. M3J 2L9
Tel: (+416) 736 6111
Fax: (+416) 736 6112
www.diamondyarn.com

NORWAY
Du Store Alpakka AS
Mohagasvingen 4,
2770, Jaren.
Tel: (+47) 61 32 70 90
www.dustorealpakka.com

SPAIN/FRANCE/GERMANY/ LUXEMBOURG/BELGIUM/ HOLLAND
Katia
Av. Catalunya, s/n-08296,
Castellbell I el Vilar (Barcelona).
Tel: (+34) 93 834 02 01
www.katia.es
France
Tel: (+34) 93 834 10 88

GERMANY
Designer Yarns (Deutschland) GmbH
Sachsstrasse 30,
D-50259, Pulheim Brauweiler
Tel: (+49) 2234 205453
Fax: (+49) 2234 205456
www.designeryarns.de

UNITED KINGDOM
Designer Yarns Ltd
Units 8-10 Newbridge Industrial Estate,
Pitt Street,
Keighley,
West Yorkshire
BD21 4PQ
Tel: (+44) 01535 664222
Fax: (+44) 01535 664333
Email: alex@designeryarns.uk.com
www.designeryarns.uk.com

Websites
The Mirasol Yarn Collection website:
www.mirasolperu.com

Jane Ellison's website:
www.janeellison.co.uk

acknowledgements

There are many talented and gifted people who have lent their skills to the production of this book. Getting a knitting book together is never easy and has lots and lots of intricate details that need dedication and, most importantly, a love of your work to complete. Thank you to all of you who have worked so hard, especially Luise, to get this book together and made it fun to work on.

I am grateful to Sion Elalouf from Knitting Fever for asking me to design and be so involved with the MIrasol Yarn Collection and recognising that this would be something very close to my heart. A special thank you also to Peter Mulley from Diamond Yarn and Raul Rivera from Michell for all their support. And, a special acknowledgement to Kari Hestnes who, to me, is the mother of the Mirasol Project.

Thank you to my knitters who constantly produce hand knits to a fantastic standard within very tight deadlines. Your talents and commitment to making high quality garments is amazing.

credits

The publisher would like thank pattern checker Marilyn Wilson, Luise Roberts for her excellent editorial and design input, and models Joanna Heygate, Luisa Savoia and Melissa Spencer.